HYPE!

HYPE!

The
Essential
Guide
to
Marketing
Yourself

Andrew Crofts

Hutchinson
Business
Books

First published in Great Britain by
Hutchinson Business Books Limited
An imprint of Random Century Limited
Random Century House
20 Vauxhall Bridge Road, London SWIV 2SA

Random Century Australia (Pty) Limited
20 Alfred Street, Milsons Point,
Sydney, NSW 2061, Australia

Random Century New Zealand Limited
9-11 Rothwell Avenue, Albany
Private Bag, North Shore Mail Centre
Glenfield, Auckland 10, New Zealand

Century Hutchinson South Africa (Pty) Limited
PO Box 337, Bergvlei 2012, South Africa

British Library Cataloguing in Publication Data
Crofts, Andrew
    Hype!
    1. Business enterprise. Success
    I. Title
    650.1

ISBN 0-09-174543-8
ISBN 0-09-174542-X pbk

Typeset in Bembo by SX Composing Ltd, Rayleigh, Essex
Printed and bound in Great Britain by
Mackays of Chatham PLC, Chatham, Kent

Contents

Introduction			vii
Chapter	1	Starting with trade media	1
	2	Moving into consumer media	16
	3	Giving yourself a USP	26
	4	Taking to the stage	29
	5	On to the airwaves	43
	6	The power of the small screen	47
	7	Publishing a book	61
	8	Using your lifestyle	74
	9	Creating the right image	80
	10	Being talked about	87
	11	Coping with scandal	92
	12	Myth and mystery	96
	13	Professional help	100
		Summary	106
		Index	108

Introduction

MOST OF US dream sometimes of being famous: the young management consultant sits reading books and articles about high-flyers and watching Tom Peters videos; the would-be actress in the darkened cinema, watching her heroines on the big screen.

Not all of us can hope to reach such giddy heights, but there is only one sure way to fail – and that is never to try at all. Aim for the sky, and at least you may end up at the top of a tree; aim for nothing, and that's almost certainly what you'll end up with. Combined with your will and commitment to success, this book can take you from total obscurity to world-wide fame.

Of course, you may not *want* to reach the glories of the last few chapters: there are many levels of fame which offer great rewards – both mental and material. You may simply want to write articles and books, go on the speaking circuit or appear on television because you think it would be fun. Or you might have a very serious business plan, part of which relies on you becoming a widely-known expert in your field.

You may well wish to treat the whole search for fame as something of a game; a chase to be enjoyed for its own sake, with the final achievement as simply the icing on the cake. On the other hand, you might have decided that the only way to achieve the lifestyle you want is to become rich and influential, and that the only way to do that in your profession is to become famous first.

Whatever your ambition, reading this book will give you a clearer idea of the options open to you, and will enable you to develop a plan that suits you for raising your profile.

Not everyone who has achieved fame has followed all the steps which I have outlined, or in the sequence in which I have organized them. Some might have found fame 'overnight' with the publication of a book or the production of a television programme. Some people might have had fame thrust upon them by accident and are now looking for ways to exploit and prolong it. But whatever your particular circumstances, *there has never been a better time to become famous.* The media grows wider and more diverse almost daily, and the global village which Alvin Toffler predicted is becoming a reality in many industries and professions. English is growing more and more dominant as the international business language, so if you can read this book, you are already in an advantageous position for building a reputation that spans the world.

Good luck.

CHAPTER ONE

Starting with Trade Media

THIS BOOK IS about a marketing campaign in which you are the product. You are also, of course, the marketeer – a situation with some advantages, and some potential problems. It means that you have almost total power to shape the product, and it means that you don't have to consult anyone else about how you do it, or even take their opinions into account. Consequently, if you make some bad judgments, there may not be anyone else to advise you or to share the blame.

The whole point of self-marketing is to draw attention to yourself, which means you could be drawing attention to your mistakes as well as your triumphs. The public likes to build people up, and then knock them down. Today you may be the most fashionable of gurus in your field, tomorrow you may be dubbed old-fashioned. You must be prepared to weather the downs as well as the ups.

In a *corporate* marketing campaign there are lengthy meetings at every stage of the operation. The campaign might start with the conception of the product, then go through the design phase, testing processes, packaging and sales promotion ideas, pricing and financial planning, distribution, advertising and after-sales services. All these matters are discussed in great depth at every stage, and a number of minds are put to solving each problem as it arises. By the end of the campaign, many of the team members involved at the beginning may have left. With the building of your own reputation there will be no such chance of escaping: you will reap the rewards and pay the penalties for all the decisions you make along the way.

In your campaign to market yourself you may have no-one to call upon for objective advice and moral support. Of course, if you are already in a position of some influence, you may have the services of a public relations consultancy with a brief which includes raising your personal profile as part of a larger corporate public relations effort.

The chances are, however, that you are on your own and that your colleagues at work will be trying to build their own reputations and won't be interested in giving you any good advice (in fact they might even have a vested interest in holding you back: anyone who stands out from the crowd often kindle jealousy and envy in the hearts of others, particularly if they are believed to be actively courting the publicity). You must learn how to promote yourself as you go along without much help from others.

If you are aiming high, you will have to work hard at your reputation, making sure that you are skilled at being famous once you get there, and that you have the knowledge and ability to back up your reputation. As Andy Warhol once predicted, all sorts of people can become famous for 15 minutes – but only those who have done the right groundwork can sustain that fame and build on it.

For most of you, the trade media of your particular industry is the best place to start building a reputation. These publications are the ones most specifically interested in you, and most in need of fresh material – and there is your marketing opportunity.

THE PRESS BOOM

During the 1970s and 1980s the trade press enjoyed an unprecedented boom. Not only did almost every industry sprout two or three publications to serve different audiences within it, but every special interest or hobby followed suit. There is also another raft of publications which travels laterally across the business world. A managing director of an oil company may not only read the oil industry trade press, but also the management and financial publications, as will managing directors in every other industry. Whether you are an accountant, a salesperson, a lawyer or a marketing manager, there are titles aimed at you as a job title as well as those concerned with your particular industry. If you want to, you can become famous both as an oil industry expert and a management systems expert.

WHAT DO EDITORS NEED?

The problem for most editors of specialized media is finding enough material to fill their pages, particularly if their publication appears weekly. They are given a certain number of pages to cover in each issue – the number dictated by the amounts of space which have been sold by their advertising departments – and have to try to make those pages as interesting and as relevant as possible in order to keep the readers they have and to entice new ones.

Trade publishing is a very lucrative business. The more competitive the market-place becomes, the more publishers have to concentrate on coming up with good products. The days when each magazine in each sector had its own little monopoly and could afford to fill its pages with unreadably dull and irrelevant material are gone.

Trade press editors also need writers. Although the majority have a pool of freelance journalists with which to supplement their regular staff, they are always on the lookout for writing talent. The time of in-house staff on a magazine is often taken up with fitting together news stories and diary columns. Anyone who shows themselves keen to take over one or more of the features, and is known to be capable of writing to a sufficiently high standard, is likely to be welcomed. Editors of trade media need 'industry sources', i.e. people they can contact for comments on stories; people who can be relied on to say something intelligent, interesting and, hopefully, different. You can actively develop a reputation as a spokesperson for your industry by writing articles for the trade press, rather than simply waiting for journalists to 'come across you' because of your position in the industry.

Anyone who is very successful in their job will eventually build up a reputation within their industry, and will become known by the media which covers that industry. The problem is that by the time that has happened naturally, i.e. by the time you have reached the top of your profession, you may not have as much need for the publicity as you had on the way up. You may even have to start avoiding it because of pressures on your time. To make publicity work to your advantage, and in order to speed your rise to eminence, you need to draw yourself and your expertise to the attention of the editors while you are on the way up, not merely to confirm that you have got there.

The fourth thing editors need is accurate information. They need this in order to demonstrate to their readers that they are truly 'inside the industry', and to gain an advantage over the opposition. By providing it, you will soon become known as a good 'source' for quotes. That information might be facts and figures from research which you or your company have done, or a particularly interesting case study of an individual job you have undertaken, or a profile of an industry sector which you are active in as a supplier. It might be gossip about who is joining what company and why, or who has won a particular contract, which an editor can use as a news story.

START WITH THE IDEAS

Unless you come up with some ideas you have got nothing to sell to editors. So you must start by giving yourself a product in the form of a list of ideas which you can suggest as possible features or news stories. You can't have too many of these and there only have to be relatively small differences in angle between them.

The golden rule is to think, 'What do I know that would be useful for others to know?' You also need to think what it is about your job, your company or your industry which is of most interest to people who know nothing about the subject. When you tell people what you do at a dinner party, what sort of questions do they ask? If you are in the business of running an aircraft chartering company, for instance, you might come up with the following list:

1. How are the costs of chartering made up? How much do fuel, staff and hire of aircraft, etc. cost?

2. How are companies using chartering to move their executives around faster?

3. How much money can companies save by using charter flights for their managers as opposed to scheduled ones – savings in hotels because of flexibility, etc?

4. What are the pros, cons and costs of chartering planes to take employees on incentive trips?

5. How do you organize an international tour for a pop star?

6. Are there places which are inaccessible to other forms of transport, but where it is possible to land charter planes?

7. What sort of planes are becoming available through chartering and how do they compare in comfort, speed and cost with scheduled flight planes?

8. What are the advantages and disadvantages of using helicopters as opposed to fixed-wing aircraft?

9. Should companies think of running their own corporate aircraft, and if so, what are the likely costs?

10. Is there a need for greater regulation (or greater deregulation – whatever the case is) in the charter airline industry?

11. Is finding cabin staff a problem in the charter airline industry?

12. Do charter airline cabin staff need special training?

13. What is the industry's future – what are the opportunities for growth, and what are the possible dangers?

This list could probably be doubled or quadrupled by someone who actually works in the charter airline industry. Some of the questions could be answered simply with the information in that person's head, while some would require research.

RESEARCHING YOUR TARGET AUDIENCE

The next question is how to market these ideas to your first target audience – the trade press editors. You must decide which of the many magazines in the market you are going to aim for. There may just be one or two that you want to get into, in which case you need to be very careful in getting the product right before you approach them, because you will soon run out of options. In most cases, however, there will be more than that, so you will need to draw up a 'hit list' in order of priority, and start to keep a careful record of exactly what you are going to offer to each one.

Start by reading the publications carefully for a few weeks. See how they are divided into different sections. Think about the kinds of people they are aimed at and what potential readers will expect to gain from reading their pages. Would your ideas fit well into their general features pages? Or do they run 'special features' which your ideas would be more suited to? Is there a regular 'Comment' column written by someone from the industry for which you would be able to tailor one of your ideas?

Once you are familiar with the layout of the magazine, find out who is responsible for which divisions. If the publication is very small, it's possible that the editor does everything. The chances are, however, that there will be someone working as Features Editor, someone else as News Editor and, if the publication is of reasonable size, a Special Features Editor as well. On a major publication these people may even have deputies or assistants and you won't need to go any higher than them. Always start at the bottom: if there is a personality clash with an assistant editor, you can always try approaching their boss later. Fall out or disagree with the boss at the start and you can't then approach an assistant.

You will usually find all the staff's names listed in the 'masthead' of the magazine (the 'who's who' list usually found on the first inside page), or you may have to ring and ask who is the right person to approach. Check that you have the right address: many magazines operate from several different addresses, with advertising at one, subscriptions at another and editorial at a third.

PROVING YOURSELF

The two things that editors need to know about you are: (a) can you write, and (b) are you reliable?

The better you can write, the less time and trouble the staff will have to go to when editing what you send in. It may be that what you have to say is so good that a few grammatical errors or spelling mistakes won't matter. On the whole, however, it is not worth taking the risk. Don't forget that they will be judging your general competence as a commentator on your industry from what you send them; so you need to take some care over presentation if you want to maintain your credibility.

You need to prove your reliability in two ways. Firstly, you must show that you can be relied on to write accurately and not to get things wrong. If you talk rubbish and they publish what you write in good faith, it will be their magazine which will be branded as not knowing what it is talking about. So do your research thoroughly.

Secondly, they need to know that you can be relied on to get an article to them when you say you will, or preferably earlier. An enormous number of people promise editors that they will write something. The editor leaves room on the pages, and may even tell the advertising department, who will sell space on the back of the idea. When the final deadline arrives, the editor finds that the would-be contributor just hasn't got round to writing the piece, and that another piece – perhaps of a much lower standard than the one that was expected – has to be hurriedly commissioned, or even dug out from a 'back up' pile. Never promise an article to an editor until you are sure that you can deliver it, and always make the writing of it your first priority as soon as it has been asked for. Find out when the deadline is, but don't leave the writing to the last minute – you may fall sick or suddenly be sent abroad and be unable to write it. You only have to let an editor down once for him or her not to want to risk using you again.

The best way to alleviate an editor's fears and to prove that you are up to the job, is to start by writing an article before you have contacted anyone. Choose one of the ideas on your list – either one which you know you are already an expert on, or one which would be useful for you to research anyway – and write the piece with a particular magazine in mind so that you know how long it should be and what kinds of people it should address. Type the piece neatly on one side of A4 paper, double-spaced with wide margins: showing that you know the professional rules will help you to win the editor's confidence.

OVERCOMING WRITER'S BLOCK

Many people who have never written an article (as well as some who write regularly) find themselves daunted by the sight of a blank sheet of paper. *Don't give up.* There are a number of ways of overcoming the feeling. The golden rule is just to start writing. Stop thinking about the perfect way to phrase your thoughts and just get them down on paper, or on the screen, in any old order. It doesn't matter how badly written the result is because you now have something to work with and can correct it or even completely re-write it.

If you really can't get a single word on to paper, then change track. Get a tape recorder and talk your thoughts into it, just as if you were describing what you want to say to another person. You can then transcribe this and start to prune and improve what appears on the paper in front of you.

Another way to get going is to list all the questions you are going to answer, then write a paragraph on each, gradually building up the different arguments or examples, and then joining them as a whole to make the article 'flow'.

STARTING WITH TRADE MEDIA

In some cases the material for your article may already exist in another form and will simply need adapting. If, for instance, you have just given a speech at a conference, you might be able to turn it into an article with a minimum of work. If your company has just conducted a survey into some issue of importance to the company and its industry sector, that too might easily convert into a useful and interesting article.

It doesn't matter how you do it, as long as something gets written, and as long as you are confident at the end that it is the best you can do. Nor does it matter how long it takes because you are not working to a deadline at this stage, you have only yourself to satisfy. Be sure, however, that it is progressing all the times. The danger is that you will tell yourself that you are 'thinking about it' in preparation for writing it, when in fact you are merely putting off the day when you have to sit down and do it.

Once you start writing, the ideas will usually flow and you will find that you can do in a few hours what you thought was going to take weeks – and what may take months if you continue to procrastinate.

SELLING WHAT YOU'VE WRITTEN

Once you have a written article, there are two main choices open to you. One is to send the completed piece to the editor at the top of your list; the other is to send him or her a synopsis of it. A synopsis must be sufficiently detailed to demonstrate that you have enough material and that you have thought it through sufficiently clearly. Always send a covering letter with it asking if he or she would like to see the completed article and explaining why you think it might be of interest to him or her. Enclose a stamped, self-addressed envelope in which the editor can return it to you if it is unsuitable.

Now, simply sit back and wait. Don't keep pestering the magazine; but if you haven't heard from them in two weeks, telephone to check that the article has arrived and ask if they think it might be of use to them.

COPING WITH REJECTION

If your article is rejected, ask the editor if he or she would like any other ideas for articles, or if the magazine has any features planned which you might be able to help with. The chances of them turning you down completely are very small; they are more likely to suggest that you send in a few more ideas (they might even ask you for a few over the telephone, so have your list to hand).

If possible, try to find out why the article was judged unsuitable, without wasting too much of their time or aggravating them with a detailed cross-examination. You need to know whether it was the idea itself which didn't fit their plans, or your writing style. If it was the latter, then you need to find out where you are going wrong. Always welcome criticism. It is the only way you will learn how to do the job better. If you become defensive, arrogant or over-sensitive, people won't bother to tell you why you are failing to get into print, and you will be discouraged.

If your article has been rejected on the grounds that the idea didn't fit, send it immediately to the next magazine on your list and repeat the process. Even if this initial article never gets into print, at least you are beginning to get to know the editors and finding out what their needs are.

If the first editor has agreed to see some more ideas, send in your three best ones, explaining briefly why you think the magazine's readers might be interested in each of them. Telephone again in a couple of weeks if you have heard nothing, and offer to send more ideas if those ones weren't suitable. At this stage there is no substitute for perseverence. Even if the editor ends up giving you something to do simply to get you off the telephone, you have moved a step forward, because you then have the opportunity to prove how skilful you are at answering a brief.

FACE-TO-FACE MEETINGS

Many public relations experts still believe in the power of the 'lunch' to meet editors and give them stories. While a lunch-time meeting may be a pleasant way to get to know someone and cement a contact, it is not necessary at the beginning, and will merely look like a bribe. Most busy editors will resent spending time on a long lunch unless they are sure they are going to get a story from it.

There is no harm, however, in making face-to-face contact. Offer to come to the editor's office to chat about your ideas, or to drop off the manuscript. If they don't seem keen then don't insist: many regular contributors to magazines have never met their editors, conducting all their dealings on the telephone or by post.

SPECIAL REPORTS

More and more magazines are using the 'special report' format. It is generally instigated by the advertising departments, who want to persuade advertisers to buy space in particular issues. The marketing press, for instance, carries special features on conferences, incentives, sales promotion, direct marketing, and so forth.

A special feature has to carry several articles on the same subject if it is to have any credibility. This means that editors (or Special Features Editors in the case of larger publications) have to keep coming up with a number of articles in ever-more specialized areas. This is an ideal opportunity to offer your assistance.

Find out what special features are coming up. Most advertising departments now publish lists a year in advance, so telephone for one of these: if you sound like a potential advertiser you will have no problem getting one sent to you (you may also get some advertising sales calls afterwards, but that is a small price to pay). If you are known to be a potential contributor, then the editorial department may also send you a list.

There are companies which sell regular up-dates of all the special features coming up in the next few months across the whole media, but it is not worth subscribing to one of these unless you are in the public relations business and have a broad range of possible subjects that you are interested in publicizing.

If you know exactly what headings your subject of expertise falls into, then you can simply contact the magazine and ask them when the next feature on that subject is coming up.

There are sometimes overlaps of interest between different features. An article originally destined for a conferences feature, for instance, might end up in a feature on visual aids, or audio-visual equipment. As far as you are concerned the important thing is to get the trade press to accept your piece – what they do with it is up to them.

Always bear in mind that magazines are planned many months in advance. It is no good approaching an editor the week before a special feature is due to appear: they will probably already have printed it. How far ahead they are working will depend on whether they publish monthly or weekly; but as a rule it is never too soon to start suggesting ideas.

WILL YOU BE PAID?

As a basic rule editors pay when they know that the writer earns a living from writing and not from public relations, and when they have to approach the writer rather than the other way round.

As far as using media to enhance your reputation is concerned, money is of secondary importance at this stage. The important thing is to get published and to build a profile within the media. It is therefore best not to mention the subject at all unless the editor does.

Once the relationship is established, however, and you are known to be a good source of material, special features editors will start approaching you with ideas for articles which you might like to write for them. While you are still more interested in being published than being paid, you can now enquire what they are willing to pay. They will have standard rates, and will probably be prepared to pay you just as they would a professional journalist. As long as it is you who is suggesting the ideas, however, it would not be very tactful to start asking for money.

AVOIDING PUFFERY

While editors are very reliant on people who have vested interests in wanting to write for their magazines, they have to be careful not to become victims of 'puffery'.

Puffery means giving obvious publicity within an article to a company or service, beyond what is necessary to explain and illustrate the arguments being made. There is a very fine dividing line between when it is and isn't acceptable, and it basically comes down to common sense and good taste. If you are writing an article about a case study, you are obviously going to mention the companies involved in the job. If, however, you are writing a general article about landscape gardening, it would be unacceptable to keep saying, 'At Bloggs and Co Landscape Gardeners we always . . .'

If an editor is receiving an article from you free of charge, he or she will expect you to promote your cause in some way, otherwise why would you do it? At this stage in building your profile, however, you should not be out for short-term plugs, either for yourself or for your company; you are looking for the best way to build a long-term reputation. A reputation for understanding a whole market-place or industry is much more valuable than a reputation for getting your company a lot of free publicity in the right media. The latter is the job of public relations companies. You are concerned with an altogether bigger project which will, as a spin-off, also benefit the company you work for.

Many magazines will, at the end of your article, put a few words to explain who you are, e.g. *John Smith is Managing Director of Bloggs Landscape Gardeners*. For the purposes of building a reputation, this is all that is necessary at this stage.

BECOMING A 'QUOTE SOURCE'

It is nearly always better to be the subject of an article rather than the writer, since the writer only gets mentioned once, in a by-line which is generally so discreet that no-one will notice it unless you point it out to them. As the subject of the article, you may be quoted several times and have your picture on the page. The very fact that you are being used as a source of quotes demonstrates that you are a respected voice within your industry, and implies a status which you may or may not yet have earned.

When a journalist starts to tackle a subject, he or she often knows nothing about it. An editor may ring one day and say, 'Could you do me 2,000 words on why companies are starting to use video conferencing for international meetings?' The journalist agrees and the editor suggests a few people who might be worth talking to. When the article appears, the people that the journalist has talked to will probably have their pictures in the article, and will appear to be the leading experts on their subject.

So how can *you* become one of the people whose name gets given to the journalists when they are commissioned to write the articles? You will already have done some of the groundwork by becoming known for the articles you have written. If you have already written a piece about the rising costs of holding international meetings, you are obviously going to be able to contribute to the video conferencing subject. Likewise, if you have written something about developments in television technology, you are going to be able to answer some of the journalist's questions.

Secondly, you may have become known through the distribution of press releases and news stories via your company's public relations consultancy or department.

The only way to *ensure* that you are the one who is called upon is to be in continual contact with magazine editors, and with as many as possible of the writers they use regularly.

When, for instance, you are talking to the Special Features Editor about articles you could possibly write for a particular feature, you should ask what other subjects are being covered in the same feature and offer your assistance to the writers involved. You should try to find out who the individual writers are and telephone them to offer your help. If they show the slightest interest, then suggest that you send them more information, and let them have as much as possible as quickly as possible, so that when they come to put together the piece they have all your material in front of them.

Offer to meet writers, for lunch if necessary, in order to expand on what you have been saying, or perhaps to show them round your works or give them a demonstration of the equipment they are writing about. If they don't have time to meet, don't be insistent; just answer their questions as clearly and honestly as possible over the telephone, and leave them with your telephone number, asking them to contact you if they need any more information.

Try to get the addresses of any freelance writers whose articles you read, so that you can keep them informed of what you are doing and where you can be contacted should they be doing another story along similar lines. Most writers will do more than one article on any subject they have become interested in, and may well need more quotes a month – or even a year – after the initial contact.

As soon as any article you have helped with appears, write and thank the journalist personally, repeating your offer of lunch or a meeting. Keep a detailed contact list of anyone who has written anything about you, and watch for their name in other publications. Staff journalists move between magazines fairly frequently, and may also moonlight for other publications while holding down full-time jobs.

BEING QUOTED OUT OF CONTEXT

The only drawback to being quoted in articles is that you have no control over how your quotes are used. When you are writing an article yourself, you can continue to edit and hone it until it says exactly what you want it to say. In a five-minute telephone conversation you are likely to say all sorts of things which may be taken out of context or used wrongly in some way. There is nothing you can do about this, apart from learning by experience how to express yourself more concisely. Don't bother to ask the writer to send you a copy of the article before it goes to press – the chances are he or she will say no, or will say yes and not do it, or even feel insulted that you don't trust him or her.

If you are worried that someone may have misunderstood what you said, write to them to 'confirm' what it was that you said on the telephone.

On the whole it is better to be written about wrongly (to misquote Oscar Wilde) than not to be written about at all. If you are misquoted so badly that you are likely to be sued by someone or look incompetent, then send a letter putting the record straight, to be published in the next issue of the magazine. The chances are, however, that very few people will realize that you have been misquoted, and if they do notice, they certainly won't remember a week later. All they will remember is that they saw you written about in a magazine somewhere – that is good enough at the moment.

If you are going to put yourself forward as a source of quotes, then you must be prepared to talk honestly and not become coy with information, saying things like, 'No comment'. If there is a confidentiality problem about something you have told a journalist, don't tell him or her it's 'off the record'; just explain your problem and trust the journalist not to let you down. If the subject is so sensitive that you can't take that sort of risk, then you are probably in a job or an industry which will never allow you to have a high personal profile, at least not until you change jobs.

The ultimate success within the trade press is a complete written profile. This, however, is something you must earn; editors are unlikely to be impressed by people who continually put themselves forward as subjects for profiles.

If you have a public relations department or consultancy, they might suggest your name to editors for this sort of treatment. But the most reliable way to secure it is to work steadily towards gaining a reputation which will lead to profiles without you having to ask for them.

GETTING INTO THE NEWS

Many people's first appearance in the trade media is on the news pages. Most of the news emanates from companies rather than individuals, so for you to begin to feature heavily you have to become your company's spokesperson, at least for your sector of the company. There may be political reasons why this is impossible. If you are a marketing manager, for instance, and your marketing director likes to be the one who is quoted in press releases, there is not very much you can do about it, except to keep working at your features ideas until the news pages begin to pick up your name automatically.

You can, however, make sure that when a story relates directly to you, a press release goes out to the relevant media. If you receive a promotion, or win an incentive prize, or give a talk at a conference, you will become the subject of a potential news story; so don't allow the opportunity to pass by.

If you are already the company spokesperson, then concentrate your efforts on getting as many stories as possible out with quotes from you, and with your name and number displayed for anyone who wants to follow the story up.

You can also make yourself available for comment on wider-ranging news stories. If you are in the computer software business and a rival computer company makes an announcement which will effect the whole industry, you should quickly issue a release with your comments on what the announcement will mean to the industry, so that the journalists who are writing up the story (probably using the computer company's press release) can balance it with comments from other 'experts' in the field.

News stories are breaking every day, and you must be careful not to swamp magazines with your opinions. It might be an idea to ration yourself to one comment a month to start with. If that proves successful, start building it up. Before long you will find that magazines are ringing you for your comments without waiting for you to approach them, particularly if you are controversial and outspoken.

YOUR FACE IN THE PRESS

A picture is worth a thousand words: it's a cliché, but it's true. Most of us don't have enough time to read all the magazines which might be relevant to us. Instead, we flick through them, taking in headlines, pictures and captions. If your picture is continually appearing in the media, people will notice it, even if they never read the articles which you are mentioned in.

Being the author of an article may be enough to get your picture published (it depends on the design policy of the magazine), and people who might never have noticed your by-line will suddenly be aware that you are an authority on your subject.

If you are interviewed at length by a journalist from a magazine with a decent photography budget, they may come and take your picture specially to illustrate the story. If this happens, get the number and address of the photographer so that, if you like the results, you can buy some more copies of the picture for future use.

If you want a high profile, you will have to have some pictures done for your own use, and the more imaginative they are the more magazines are going to want to use them. You must have a basic set of black and white prints available at all times, and some colour transparencies as well just in case an opportunity arises and a magazine asks for them (if your picture appears in colour while those of your competitors are merely in black and white, readers will draw automatic conclusions about who is the most important person in the article).

The most expensive part of any photographic operation is having the sitting done; get as many different poses as possible at one go, and then order a lot of prints and distribute them generously.

Editors need pictures to fill space and enliven long articles – always give them what they want. The more imaginative the pictures and the broader the focus, the more ways they can be used. A full-length picture of you standing in a palm-filled office foyer can be cropped to 20 different shapes and sizes; a close-up of your face can only be used one way.

Add a caption to all photographs. Do not write directly on to the back of the picture as the writing will come through to the other side; tape a slip of paper to the back of the picture telling the sub-editors who you are, so that they will spell your name and the name of your company correctly when they come to write the captions.

Whenever you submit an article or a press release to a publication, include a picture. When you are talking to journalists about a story, ask them if they need pictures, and send them whatever they ask for – including a picture of yourself whether they ask for it or not. If the article is being written by a freelance journalist, ask him or her for the the name of the editor they are dealing with, and send the pictures direct to the editor, with a covering letter explaining which story they are to go with and the name of the journalist who asked for them.

Don't expect pictures to be used every time you send them. They will often be filed and you will find them popping out at a later date to illustrate the smallest of quotes which you might have made, or a news item about your company which you didn't even know was going to appear. The more pictures you have in circulation, the better the chance that they will be picked up. If the pictures you have taken are good enough, they will continue to serve you for anything up to ten years, although it will never hurt to do new ones every year or two.

WHAT TO DO NEXT

The first time you have an article published in a magazine, either by you or about you, you may be disappointed to find that it doesn't change your life. Hardly anyone seems to notice, or if they do, they neglect to tell you how clever you are.

Do not despair, the most difficult bit is over. Now that you actually have the article in its final, published form, you can use it to move on to the next stage of the race.

It has to be said that very few people actually read the articles that appear in trade papers. As we said, there are those who flick through and look at the pictures, and perhaps pick out one or two articles in each issue to read, but there are just as many who will never open the magazines at all because they don't have time. Those who do read the articles may not notice your name, and almost certainly won't remember it.

So what, you might ask, has been the point of the whole exercise? The point has been to establish that you are someone whose opinions are worth listening to, someone who is willing and able to speak out and who understands the business they are operating in. Now that the article has been published, you can have copies made (or buy 'run-ons' from the publishers if there is a copyright problem) and distributed to relevant target audiences. Although people may not take much notice of an article when it is part of a magazine, they *will* notice it when it is extracted and brought to their attention with a covering note.

It's a good idea to send a copy to editors of other publications to demonstrate that you are already a published writer, which means that with them you will not have to go through the initial stages of proving your abilities. You might like to send copies to organizers of conferences and seminars in case they are looking for new speakers in your field.

Your achievement represents the first brick in the wall of your reputation.

CHAPTER TWO

Moving into
Consumer Media

LIKE TRADE PUBLISHING, the consumer press burgeoned during the 1980s. Where once there were a handful of powerful daily papers and weekly women's magazines, there are now a plethora of titles serving almost every possible market niche. Where once a few mighty local papers straddled the counties, there are now a host of 'freebies' competing with them for space on the average suburban doormat.

For someone who wants to be famous this has advantages and disadvantages. The disadvantage is that with so many new titles being launched all the time, the competition for readers' time is growing. At one time, if you were written about in *The Times* and the *Daily Telegraph*, you could feel confident that the majority of the middle classes would read about you. If you wanted to talk to the workers, you got into the *Daily Mirror*. Now, there are just too many pages carrying too many stories for anyone to be able to make a big impact. Unless you are front page news it is going to take you longer than ever before to hack your way through the jungle of newsprint and bring yourself to the attention of the information-sated general public.

The advantage is that with so much media, someone who keeps chipping away at it will find far more potential outlets for themselves as they make their way up the ladder. It's like lighting a stubborn fire: you keep applying matches to different parts, only to see the initial flicker of flame die away; but eventually, through perseverence (and a whole box of matches), the logs catch and the whole thing takes off.

Persistence is the only answer. Only by continually coming up with new ideas and new approaches will you be able to work your way into the public consciousness for more than a few days at a time. Even front page stories fade in the memory if the fire isn't continually stoked and the flames fanned when they look like dying away.

Of course, you may only want to go as far as the local media. If, for instance, you are a retailer with only one outlet in a provincial town, there is little value to be had from appearing in the national press, but a great deal from being in the local papers every week.

The women's media which, despite all the changes wrought by feminism over the 70s and 80s, remains strictly gender-bound and full of subjects which are supposed to be of interest only to women, although research suggests that a great many men also read the magazines, even if they don't buy them. The 'women's pages' of the national papers fit more easily with the women's magazines as part of a target market, than with the other contents of the newspapers.

The business press consists of some very glossy business magazines which only just pull themselves out of the 'trade' category, the business pages of all the nationals (and some women's magazines as well), plus lots of marginal material, like in-flight and railway magazines, which border on 'general interest'.

The men-only category includes the sex magazines and some of the more serious sporting titles. There are now some 'lifestyle' magazines for men, based on the same formats as the more up-market women's journals.

Finally, there are the general news and features pages of the big-time national papers, which appear every day of the week and have a voracious appetite for stories and personalities, but which chew them up and spit them out as quickly as they discover them. To be able to stay on these buckling broncos for any length of time, you have to be a very experienced rider indeed, and it would be sensible to start with some of the gentler categories first, before heading for the big-time.

STARTING LOCAL

The local press is like a microcosm of the nationals. It works to similar criteria and has similar problems, just on a smaller scale. Local papers are an excellent place to gain experience in media relations, since most people in business are going to be bigger fish in smaller ponds than they could hope to be in the national arena. Give a hundred pounds to a charity and you may well get your picture on the front page of a local paper, but you are unlikely to get into the nationals.

If you are in a service industry, then you may be able to obtain a regular slot in a local paper as an adviser to readers. If, for instance, you run an auction room, you could write a column each week valuing people's furniture and jewellery. If you are a builder's merchant, you could provide a DIY column, telling people how to lag their roofs or lay crazy paving. If you are an estate agent, you could write on how to improve the value of your property, how to make it more saleable or how to find a bargain. The list is endless, but success will depend on how well you can write and on whether you can persuade an editor to carry the material.

As with the trade press, it's best to start by writing an article in the style which you think is suitable, just to prove you can do it. It doesn't need to be long – 500 words is quite adequate. Find out the name of the editor and send the article in with a covering letter explaining that you would like to make it a regular service, perhaps answering readers' letters.

Go to one paper at a time (starting with the largest circulation and working downwards), and make it clear that you don't expect to be paid for the service.

You may, or may not, be able to get a mention of your company in the by-line of each article, but that is not the primary objective. The objective is to get your own name well-known as an expert on your subject. Once you are established as 'the financial expert' from the local paper, you can use the title in any way you like: for winning new business, getting a new job, giving talks to groups of potential customers, talking on local radio . . . all things we will discuss later.

Because most local papers appear weekly at the most, the pressures to meet deadlines are not too heavy, and anyone giving advice will have plenty of time to look up anything they don't know, and to check that the information they are giving out is correct.

Once the column has been running for a while, you can put together a collection of the best ones and start sending them to other publications, suggesting this time that people pay you for your services. You might want to upgrade to a better local paper with a wider circulation, or to a trade paper. You might even be able, with a good collection of cuttings, to move into a national consumer publication, or persuade a publisher that you should write a book. A gardening or legal correspondent could as easily be working for a women's magazine as a local paper – the first step is simply to prove that you can do it.

Although it is going to be easier to persuade an editor that you are capable of such a job if you are the proprietor of a business, there is no reason why you shouldn't be able to do the same even if you are still a humble employee. If you are a qualified solicitor working in someone else's practice, there is no reason why you shouldn't write a legal advice column under your own name. It is then up to your bosses whether they want the company name to be associated with your success or not. (If they are not encouraging, the chances are that you are going to be moving on to a new job fairly soon anyway, since they obviously do not have your best career interests at heart.) The same applies for someone working in a financial services operation, or a garden centre. If you feel you have the knowledge to advise people, and the ability to write interesting copy, then it is never too soon to start.

It may be difficult to draw the line between writing an advice column to build a reputation which will further your career, and becoming a full-time writer of advice columns. The only way to find where the line should go is to measure the amount of time it is taking you to do the self-promotion. If you are finding it hard to do your real job because of the time you are spending writing columns for magazines, you may have got the balance wrong – alternatively you may be more suited to journalism than whatever else it is you are doing; you must decide how to balance your efforts most effectively.

Taking up a 'good cause'

Another way of getting on to the pages of local papers is the taking up of a 'good cause'. It may sound cynical to advocate using a good cause for your own career furtherment, and perhaps it is, but it is a method which has long been used by politicians; and whatever your motives, it does at least benefit the cause concerned. You must, however, be sincere in your intention to help, as well as in your intention to win publicity, otherwise your insincerity will shine through and the project will fail.

Which cause to take up depends on your own interests and the needs of your neighbourhood. Whatever the project, you need to be prepared to give up time and a great deal of energy on fund raising, petition signing and campaigning – as well as making sure that you are always the spokesperson for the cause.

Become friendly with the picture desks of local papers, so that they can send photographers when you tell them you have a story for them: editors of local papers always need pictures of local people to enliven their stories.

Once you have built a relationship with a paper, you will have won their trust and be able to go to them with stories about yourself. You might be opening a business or a new branch; you might be celebrating a year in business, reaching a magic figure like one million pounds in sales or welcoming the thousandth customer through your doors. Whatever it is, it will be easier to persuade the editor to send a journalist and photographer if you are already a well-known local figure.

Being spokesperson for your industry

When writing in the trade press, you will only really be seen as a spokesperson for your company or for yourself. Once you move into the consumer media you will start to be viewed as a spokesperson for your industry.

Some industries of course, like some ministries, get called on for comment a great deal, while others have lower profiles. The spokesperson for the tobacco industry is likely to be called upon to comment on health and moral issues virtually daily without having to search for opportunities, whereas the spokesperson for the filing cabinet industry will have to work at creating a need for comment.

Every industry, however, is going to provide opportunities for self-promotion at some stage. Look how dull the diary market seemed, until someone invented the *filofax*.

If, for instance, you are an accountant with a company which makes filing cabinets, you might think there is little hope of developing a high profile in the media. But this is not true; it is a question of thinking laterally. High technology receives a great deal of coverage in the press, and everyone talks a great deal about the 'paperless office'. If such a development was to come to fruition, it would knock the filing cabinet industry for six. So is the industry finding the going tough, or is the paperless office a myth which will never come true? You immediately have the basis of at least an article, and at most a localized controversy.

On every newspaper there will be someone whose job it is to follow your industry. It may not be their exclusive task; you may just be one of a range of subjects which that correspondent covers. Office systems, for instance, might fall into the same basket as high technology and information systems: watch the papers for by-lines on subjects closely related to yours.

As soon as you have the name of a journalist on a story which seems relevant, you should telephone or write to him or her suggesting your ideas and asking for an opportunity to go and see him or her. Make sure you have thought your case through thoroughly, so that you won't be wasting the journalist's time. If your story is that the paperless office is a myth, then you must have the figures available to show that sales of filing cabinets are growing steadily. You must be able to back up whatever you are putting forward as a theory, so that the journalist can write the article, confident that the facts are right.

GOING NATIONAL

Often, the national media will pick up a story from the trade or local media and expand it, or pick out a key point and turn it into a news story. Don't wait for this to happen: if you have had an article published in a trade journal, send copies to all the relevant writers on consumer papers. Attach a covering letter telling them why you thought the article might be of interest to them so that they can tell at a glance whether you are on to something, without having to read through the whole text. Offer to talk to them in greater detail if they want.

Most of the quality newspapers now carry special features. Some of them are industry-based, concentrating on the metal industry or the paper industry for instance, while others zero in on a geographical area like a major city. You need to know what special features are in the pipeline so that you can approach the relevant editors with offers of help. If they are writing eight pages on Liverpool, and you happen to be a prominent Liverpool businessperson, they may well be willing to profile you. If you are already known as a spokesperson for your industry, and your industry is heavily represented in that area, they will be able to use quotes from you. You may even be able to place articles under your own name within the feature.

Becoming a news story

In most cases this boils down to indulging in a good old-fashioned publicity stunt, the sort of thing which the showbusiness fraternity have been indulging in since Barnum and Bailey, and which these days of races across the Atlantic and so forth has reached the state of high art.

To deliberately get into the news you have to do something extraordinary. It has to be a great act of courage or a great act of folly. It has to be a fulfilment of other people's dreams, at least in part, and it is probably the least subtle and most sure-fire way to gain publicity for yourself.

It almost certainly has to be something which you already want to do, otherwise you will fail to achieve it and will merely look foolish. If Jimmy Saville hadn't enjoyed walking and running for charity, he would never have been capable of reaching the finishing post. If Richard Branson did not actually relish putting his life on the line, he would never be able to travel by balloon or head his boats off into storms.

Presuming, therefore, that you have a hobby or sport which could enable you to go for a record, or raise a large amount of money for charity, you will need to link up with other people in order to build it into the sort of stunt which makes it on to the front pages of the national press.

In order to maximize the publicity you receive, you will probably need the help of some sponsors who need publicity as much as you do. You may, of course, have the resources to fund your own escapade, or be able to think of something which costs very little to do, but you are still going to need the help of somebody's corporate public relations department if you are going to get the most from the event.

If, for instance, you are planning to walk from Lands End to John O'Groats in one go, in order to demonstrate your theory that if you eat spinach you don't need sleep, there are a number of ways in which you can maximize the publicity. You will need to have a television crew with you all the way, as well as national newspaper journalists. In every town you go through, you will want to be met by local journalists, photographers and radio and television teams. It is not the sort of operation which you are likely to be able to arrange single handed. A spinach company, however, will probably be very keen to help you achieve your goal, and put the necessary resources at your disposal. If you can also talk a sportswear manufacturer and soft drinks company into helping, you have created a major event for yourself.

The example is unlikely, but the point is serious. When you know what it is that you want to achieve, look around for others who would benefit from it as much, or even more, than you. Preferably you need someone with a lot of money, which means a large company. Be sure that the project is something which you could achieve even if they didn't agree to help, otherwise you will be giving them too much power, and be clear in your mind how you are going to do it. Approach the marketing department of companies concerned to ask if they would like to participate, and make it clear that the event is going to happen one way or another, implying politely that if they aren't interested in helping, you will be going to their competitors.

One major publicity stunt, which gets you on to the front pages of the national press, should be enough to launch you on a career; but you must have a follow-up campaign prepared. You must be sure that you have material for follow-up articles, books or talks. You must be able to produce new research and new findings all the time if you are to remain prominent. People soon forget you if you drop out of the public eye, but the longer you can stay in the limelight after a major *coup*, the easier it is to get back each time with something new.

When a new young athlete wins a gold medal at the Olympics, or a pop singer makes it to number one, everyone wants to talk to them and write about them. If they are clever, and pace themselves carefully, they can build an image which will last them the rest of their lives. If they are not sufficiently prepared for sudden fame, they will disappear as quickly as they appeared. They will still have done more than most people in getting to the front pages at all, but they will not have grasped the ultimate prize of a lifetime's reputation.

Look, for instance, at the difference between Henry Cooper, with his carefully-paced career as a personality and speaker, and the hundreds of boxers, many of them better at boxing than him, who have come and gone and are only remembered by avid historians of the sport. Look at racing drivers like Stirling Moss and Jackie Stewart who may not have raced cars for years, but have managed to nurture reputations in many other ways, so that people still know what it was they were originally famous for.

Surveys and research

Just like the trade media, consumer media is always hungry for facts and figures which prove something new. If you can produce evidence, even in the spurious form of a survey which might only have sampled a hundred people, that something surprising is indeed a fact, you will be able to command the attention of journalists and editors.

You must be sure, however, that the fact is something which you want to prove, and something that you would want to continue to defend after the results are published. Unless you are obviously sincere about the work, you will soon be found out and people will lose interest.

Supposing, for instance, you are an accountant and you want to become well-known for your work with the tax authorities. You have a strongly-held belief that the majority of self-employed people who do not use the services of accountants end up paying more tax than they should. If you were to do some research on, say, a hundred sample cases, and found that your theories were right, you could soon extract some pretty stunning figures, and some good headlines like, 'Taxman cheats self-employed of a billion pounds a year'. You must, however, be prepared to go in front of the cameras and justify your findings in some detail.

Good works

We touched on this subject in the section on local media, and the same rules apply on a wider scale in the national media. If you can find a cause which you care about, and which you are willing to devote time and energy to, it will help you to lift your own reputation. By lifting your own reputation you can do even more to help the cause, and that may appease any twinges of conscience which you may have about 'cashing in' on the misfortunes of others.

The greatest case study of this is Bob Geldof, who was a pop singer on the verge of slipping out of fashion when he took up the cause of starvation in Ethiopia, forming Band Aid and all the other associated charities, which set a new fashion for giving to the Third World. He managed to make himself a world figure almost overnight, but it was only possible because everyone was convinced of his sincerity in what he was attempting to achieve. He was genuinely angry at what was happening, and he had the strength of character to do something about it.

His extreme success is unusual. He happened to be in the right place at the right time. He was able to get the top music establishment on his side, and that meant the media would follow him everywhere.

But there are many other opportunities for quieter and more modest efforts. Decide what it is that you want to achieve, and ensure that it is in line with your other ambitions. Often, people find themselves led to a cause by a family tragedy which alerts them to a

need for greater medical resources or safety procedures in some area
or other.

The public concern over the environment, which surfaced at the
end of the 1980s, has provided a host of bandwagons for people to
jump on. People now campaign to save whales, trees, polar bears
and the ozone layer. All the causes are good, some of the motives
may be suspect, but it is always better to do something than nothing.

Confrontation

For those who enjoy it, nothing guarantees publicity as much as a
good confrontation.

In the business world, battles symbolized by the personalities of
the leaders are the ones which command the front pages of the press.
Arthur Scargill leading his mine workers against Ian MacGregor and
the Coal Board; Tiny Rowland fighting for ownership of Harrods;
and Lord Forte battling for the Savoy: they are all stories which run
and run.

In most cases, it doesn't seem to matter whether you win or lose –
it is how you conduct yourself during the battle which counts for
your long-term reputation. When George Davis was ousted from
Next, a company which he was known by the public to have created
almost single-handed, the press loved him because he looked like the
small man being victimized by the anonymous figures of big
business.

If you are prepared to step out of the shadows, showing that you
are not frightened to speak your mind and voice a few of your prejudices, which are probably shared with a large part of the population,
you will always win applause. You will have to be prepared to
alienate as many people as you win, of course, but you can console
yourself that in the long run even the most frightening of bogey-men
seem to grow familiar and comfortable with age. Who is frightened
of Tony Benn or Enoch Powell now? Even Arthur Scargill is beginning to look like a character from a nostalgic television costume
drama.

Being prepared to come out scrapping is guaranted to get column
inches in the press. The people who fought the unions, like Rupert
Murdoch and Robert Maxwell, may be hated by as many people as
they are admired by, but they are certainly well-known.

The business world only really comes to the attention of the wider
general public when there is a major scandal, a takeover battle or an
acrimonious strike. Anyone who wants to build a reputation can use
these opportunities to demonstrate what they are made of to the
watching public.

It is like knights of old jousting for the crowds: there are heroes
and villains, and sometimes they change places (consider how Sir

James Goldsmith and Lord Hanson go in and out of fashion as heroes and villains, and how Stanley Kalms of Dixons changed from being a dangerous predator to an indignant prey). Some of the heroes who fight particularly valiantly become national figures, at least for a time, until fashions change or they are later shown to have feet of clay like the rest of us.

In Hollywood, it is not unknown for the publicity departments of studios to encourage two actors or actresses to play out some feud in public simply to publicize a film. Many thousands of column inches have been spent over the years speculating on just how much Bette Davis and Joan Crawford *really* hated one another; a fire in which both the actresses and the studios had a vested interest in continually fanning.

All the world loves a fight, and if you can think of a way to give them one, they will reward you with undivided attention.

Photo opportunities

As with the trade press, the national consumer media needs good pictures all the time. All the papers have considerable libraries, and should be supplied with good, well-captioned pictures whenever they are available.

If you are writing an article, or being interviewed, make sure that the editor or journalist you have been dealing with has copies of your latest pictures; send them to picture desks automatically anyway, so that they can keep them on file for times when your name crops up in a story which you know nothing about. A journalist might, for instance, be compiling a list of the ten people most likely to succeed in the business world next year: you wouldn't want to be excluded just because they didn't have a picture to hand!

Always be alert to picture opportunities. If you are organizing an event which might be worth coverage in the media, but are not confident that the papers will send anyone to it, then hire a photographer yourself, and have the pictures sent through to the appropriate news editors, with the story and your contact number attached. If you get a good picture, it will sometimes be run where the paper would never have carried the story on its own.

CHAPTER THREE

Giving Yourself a USP

AS A PRODUCT to be marketed, you must find or invent a reason for the market to buy you. You must give yourself a USP (Unique Selling Point): something that defines you as an individual and will make you different from the millions of other people in the world and the thousands who probably do the same job as you (some of them, perhaps, even better than you do).

One way to do this is through specialization. This works in all sectors of the market-place. Recently we have seen it in the retailing sector: Sock Shop, Tie Rack, Benetton, Knobs and Knockers and Knickerbox all became well known by focusing their minds on one product range, then making sure that the market-place knew they were there and knew exactly what they were selling.

In almost every walk of life, there are people who are so obviously excellent at what they do that they will automatically rise to the top and be noticed – Bernard Levin in journalism, Alan Sugar in business and Raymond Blanc in cookery are just a few examples. These people become talked about and famous almost despite themselves, simply because of the quality of their work. Some of them come up through the high profile worlds of fashion, art and showbusiness, but they can equally easily appear in the less public worlds of insurance, advertising and fish farming. Every field has its natural stars – the rest of us have to work to get to that level.

The first step is to discover where your interests lie, and how you can become an expert in some narrow corner of your field of endeavour as a prelude to widening your horizons later. It needs to be a subject which interests you because otherwise you will never manage to summon the energy or the patience to research it as fully as you will need to. If you happen to believe that the hottest subject of the moment is Rapid Application Development in the software industry, you may well be right; if the subject doesn't interest you, however, it won't be long before you are bogged down in detail and jargon, and you will grind to a halt long before you have mastered the subject. The motivation to learn your chosen subject must be strong before you start.

In all marketing situations, the truism which emerges again and again is that the product has to be right before anything else happens, and in order to get the product right you need to know what the customer needs. As a self-marketeer, you need to find a balance between your interests and what is going to be saleable.

Of course, your actual interests might lie in a number of different areas. Suppose you are an estate agent: you might be interested in helping people to do their own conveyancing or in the relative merits of timber-framed housing – is it as safe, warm and pleasant to live in as traditional brick-built housing? With in-depth research there is almost certainly scope for an expert in either area. However, for DIY conveyancing you only really have one subject, and it is not something which would naturally broaden into other areas. If timber frames are your specialization, you could write in the trade and technical press, addressing the construction, insurance and estate agency market-places, but it might not be a subject which would interest the general consumer. If a scandal appeared, (some new evidence that timber-framed buildings are a fire hazard or are not environmentally friendly because they waste wood, for instance), then you might be called upon to give an expert point of view; the scope for either subject, however, is still severely limited.

If, on the other hand, your favourite subject is the renovation of Georgian buildings, you are into a different area altogether. By making yourself an expert on all things Georgian, you could offer advice and guidance both to the trade and to the consumer. It is a specialization which contains all sorts of further sub-divisions, each of which could be a fruitful source for articles, books, lectures and all the other media for self-promotion covered in this book. There are Georgian fireplaces, Georgian doorknockers, Georgian chairs and Georgian front doors. Once you start collecting information and doing research, the list will increase, as will your own interest in the subject.

This is just one example, but in every profession there are ways of finding something which interests you and which will make your reputation through enlightened research.

HOW TO DO IT

The first way to become a specialist is to choose a specialization which fits in with your work.

If you own an antique shop, you can become an expert in any of the objects which you sell simply by talking to the people you buy from and sell to, by reading existing books on the subject and by rummaging around in museums and archives for further information.

If you are a solicitor and want to become expert in divorce law, so that you can write advice articles in the consumer media, you can learn by doing extra research for any divorce work which comes into the practice. Let it be known among your colleagues that it is a subject you are interested in and they will probably be happy to steer such jobs in your direction, especially if it means making their own workloads lighter.

If your specialist subject is something which is *not* connected with your work, then it must be a subject which is dear to your heart, which means it is probably already your hobby. It might be re-novating rocking horses, or wind-surfing in the North Sea – what-ever it is, you will become an expert by getting better at your hobby, craft or sport.

As I said at the beginning of this book, building a reputation is a long-term project; it can even turn out to be a life-time's work. So you need to choose a subject which fits into your working or home life, preferably both, and which you feel sure you are going to want to continue developing over the years. If you simply jump on to a fashionable bandwagon, the chances are that you will not be able to sustain your supposed level of interest.

The media love to pigeon-hole people, it makes it easier for them to know who to go to for comment. Take, for instance, an analyst in a major stock-broking firm. Most analysts only work in one sector. He or she will often make a special study of a relatively new sector. It may not be the only sector that he or she knows anything about, but because it is a relatively new one there will not be a great deal of com-petition in the pundit area. Every time a company in that particular sector does something dramatic which results in their shares going either up or down, the media are going to want someone to ring for comment. They will be in a hurry, they will not want to go to the press office of your company to ask who they should speak to, they are going to want to make one call to get some quotes and write their story. Make sure they have your number and a clear idea of what your specialization is. This technique can be applied in many other areas.

CHAPTER FOUR

Taking to the Stage

MOST PEOPLE WHO want to become well-known in their field of endeavour will sooner or later be required to talk to an audience. This may mean treading the boards of a theatre or speaking at a conference. For many it will be the culmination of a dream; for others it will be a nightmare which they will have to learn to endure if they are to fulfil their wider dreams. It is a skill which anyone can master if they are sufficiently determined.

Standing up and talking to an assembled group of people is a kind of 'coming out of the closet'. As long as you were writing for magazines and newspapers you were at arm's length from your audience; you had no idea whether they were lapping up your words of wisdom or hurling the magazines aside with hoots of derision (though you probably preferred to imagine the former scenario). The very fact that an editor had agreed to publish your words helped to share the burden of blame for any shortcomings in the quality of your thoughts and conclusions.

Once you are on stage, however, it is a very different matter. Everyone who comes to listen to you will know exactly who you are, and you will get a very direct feed back from them if you have not done your homework, or if your delivery is boring. Actors who work in both theatre and cinema often claim that they prefer the live theatre because of the feedback they get from the people sitting in front of them. If you have an actor inside you, you will thrive in this atmosphere, and you may turn out to be a natural star. If you are not a natural, there is still no reason why you shouldn't turn yourself into a star with a little thought and a lot of hard work.

LEARNING TO COMMUNICATE

James Martin is something of a superstar in the world of information technology. People are willing to pay $3,000 to $4,500 for tickets to his seminars, and companies pay him a daily rate of $25,000 to consult or lecture to their people. Yet he is a painfully shy man to meet off-stage. Through his writings, teachings and broadcastings he has become a multi-millionaire (having amassed a fortune of $100 million by the end of the 1980s – his first decade as a freelance guru), yet he started out as a backroom engineer and boffin for a computer company, spending more than 20 years inside the company.

He started to build his reputation by writing books on software development while still at quite a junior level in his company. Nobody else was writing on the subject at the time and by 1967 he had developed a considerable reputation within the company as a thinker and communicator. An Englishman by birth, he was asked to join his company's research institute in New York. The institute had been set up by the company to research and teach in the manner of a university, studying the great problems of the day, solving them, and then communicating the solutions to the rest of the company and to the outside world.

Fellows of the institute were expected to be able to explain what the company was discovering and developing so that the research being done in the laboratories could be put to practical use. At that stage Martin had no practical experience of public speaking: he was a working-class lad from the Midlands who had managed to get a scholarship to Oxford and now found himself on the career fast-track. Anyone who met him socially found him painfully hard to talk to unless the conversation was about information technology or the future.

He had learnt through writing books, however, how to be clear and concise, and how to distil complicated information and clarify it on the screen or on the written page – the first rule of good presentation. Yet when he stood up to talk, he still seemed a shy, awkward man; an academic who was deeply immersed in a subject which most people couldn't begin to comprehend.

His company's approach to the way they taught people was very different to the traditional ideas of schools and universities. Instead of the teachers grading the students, the students would grade the teachers. The students, after all, were nearly all highly-motivated people who had chosen to come to the classes in order to learn. If they were not coming away with the knowledge and enthusiasm they were seeking, it must be the fault of the teachers. At the end of the courses, they were asked to fill in forms which assessed the efforts and abilities of the lecturers.

Martin thumbed through the first pile of forms which were given to him after his arrival in New York with mounting horror. Phrases such as, 'Boring delivery' and 'Didn't learn anything', jumped off the pages at him. His bosses were not impressed and he could hardly blame them. They wondered if he might be happier back in some other part of the organization, but Martin was adamant that he was exactly where he wanted to be. If he wanted to stay, they said, he must improve his act.

Martin knew that it was vital for him to learn how to communicate effectively, otherwise he would never be more than a backroom boffin. He had to think of ways to gain confidence and improve his delivery. He was sure that the material he was working on was good, and he was sure that the people he was talking to would find it interesting if it was delivered in the right way. He had to start work on improving *himself*.

He studied all the great communicators he could find – from actors to academics, professors to pop singers – trying to see how they were able to hold an audience's attention, how they developed 'charisma', and then he looked at the material which he was delivering.

By this time audio-visual techniques were coming of age in the business world, and presenters were learning to work with overhead projectors and other equipment which could help to clarify messages. Martin began to think about ways in which it could be developed. Instead of just having one overhead projector, he wondered, what if he had five different ones working at once, so that he could move about between five different screens while he talked, all of which would be linked to a hand-held unit which he could control?

He knew it was no good sticking to a tightly scripted plan under these conditions. He was talking to highly intelligent audiences who would be constantly interrupting and questioning: he had to be able to answer flexibly and be in full control of everything that happened. He needed to be able to go backwards and forwards through the material with complete confidence. He had to know his subject inside out, and have complete control of the media he was using.

He went to his bosses at the institute, who declined to invest in a specially-equipped theatre just for him. They said he could have one projector, but if he wanted more he could pay for them himself. He went out and bought the necessary equipment. He set it up in one of the institute's lecture theatres, then rehearsed and practised for hours until he could move fluently from one screen to another, moving slides backwards and forwards to illustrate his points, making his ideas flow and adding touches of drama to catch the audience's attention.

During his lectures he became more aware of the people he was talking to. He learnt how to feel if he was losing their attention, and developed techniques for winning them back. He had created an early multi-media show.

To his enormous relief he discovered that now he was putting his mind to the problem, he was actually very good at it. Like a shy boy who suddenly discovers he can act, Martin blossomed out of his shell. His on-stage presence became dynamic and compelling. The phrases on the assessment forms began to change: 'Fascinating', 'Electric', 'Held my attention every step of the way', 'I suddenly understood subjects I never thought I would grasp'.

Martin had discovered that he was actually a great performer, and he loved the feeling. He loved controlling and exciting an audience and feeling them fill with enthusiasm for his ideas. He knew he had the power to set people on fire with the knowledge which he carried in his head, and his reputation began to grow within the institute.

However confident he became while performing, his off-stage personality remained the same. In front of the audiences he was positive and charismatic; afterwards he retreated into his diffident shell. He continued to work for the same company until the end of the 1970s, then launched himself into the outside world, basing his career on his books and his world seminar tours. If he had not mastered the art of communicating on stage, he would still have been successful from his writings; but it was the personal appearances which pushed him into the superstar bracket.

MATERIAL NEEDS

There are two basic lessons to be learnt from Martin's extreme success. The first is that you have to have the best possible material. If you don't have information which audiences need to know, then you have nothing to sell; and no matter how good your presentation, you will end up with disenchanted customers (unless you are simply aiming at the after-dinner speaking circuit, but to succeed there you need to have become famous already).

Once you are sure you have the material, you must work on the presentation. It is just like a theatrical performance: for a show to work it has to have a good script, but that is never enough on its own; the actors have to be rehearsed and drilled, bullied and moulded by directors and producers, until they are giving inspirational performances, or at least the closest to inspirational that they are able to get. The business presenter may be fortunate enough to come across advisers and trainers who will fill the role of directors and producers, but it is also likely that your skills will have to be self-taught.

You must learn to master technical props like lighting, costumes and sound effects, to which the business presenter can add audio-visual and video aids.

Of course, few actors become superstars immediately, and if they do, their careers probably won't be sustainable. There are certain stages which they go through on their way to the top: perhaps years of training in drama schools, jobs in back-street repertory theatres, walk-on parts which gradually build up over decades until they are sufficiently experienced and confident to handle the big time. The business speaker must do the same.

SEARCH OUT THE TRAINING

Everyone is nervous when they first stand up to speak. Any training you can get at the beginning of your career will help. Many employers are happy to arrange courses for staff, or for experts to be brought into the company to provide in-house training. Take advantage of any such opportunities even if you don't feel you need the skills immediately. All inter-personal skills help to build a confident appearance – particularly useful to someone ambitious. If training isn't offered, then go to your boss or personnel department and ask for it. If you are turned down, think about going on courses in your spare time (which will also mean paying for them yourself), or about changing company for one which is more in tune with your personal ambitions.

You can also learn by watching other experts. Attend as many conferences and seminars as possible and analyse what the speakers are doing and what is effective. Don't just listen to what they have to say, watch their movements and the way they deliver their lines. Do they stand still or walk about? Do they use their hands a lot or not at all? Do they smile? Do they catch the eye of their audiences? Do they leave long pauses? Do they ask questions and get feedback? What visual aids do they use? What do they wear? How long do they talk for? Do they shout or whisper? Are they interesting or boring? Can you remember what they have told you after you have left the room?

Try to find a style of speech delivery which suits your personality. Building some rules for yourself at the beginning, and practising them, will help you overcome any fears of speaking in public. When you speak for the first time, you will need all the techniques you can muster to get yourself through to the end of your allotted time. As you become more experienced, more confident and more relaxed, your own personality will begin to shine through and your style will improve; at the beginning, however, don't be afraid to use as many tricks and as much artifice as possible.

Don't limit your studies to speakers in your own field but look for ways to be better than them. Watch successful politicians giving speeches, and actors doing one-man shows. Watch the good newscasters and television presenters, the great preachers and teachers. All these communicators rely on their own speaking voices to put across messages. They can all teach you something.

STARTING AS A GUEST SPEAKER

Just as actors start their careers with small parts before being given their own shows, speakers need to find slots in other people's seminars and conferences at which to practise and improve their skills before they will be ready to build seminars around their own reputations.

If you work for a large company, they will probably be pleased to help you undertake this sort of activity. If, for instance, you are employed by a management consultancy, it can only be good for the company to have you speaking at management conferences. The organizers are bound to acknowledge your company's name in all the promotional literature in order to establish your credentials as a speaker, and in doing so, they reinforce the credentials of your employer in front of some key audiences.

Who to approach

Once you feel you have something worth saying, try to think of likely audiences; people who would *benefit* from your information. They will probably be either people in your own industry or discipline, or potential customers for your products or services.

If, for instance, you are a scientist employed by a major chemical company and have been working on a new sort of fertilizer, you could talk at any farming or market-gardening conference, or you could address a seminar on agricultural problems in the Third World.

The first step is to find out who organizes the relevant events and to build yourself another hit-list. Whenever you receive some promotional literature on a seminar or conference, make a point of finding out the telephone number and address of the organizers, then ring them to find the name of the person making the decisions about who the speakers should be, and write, offering your services. It's probably too late to get into the event advertised as such arrangements will already have been made, but if it is a professional company they will be using their expertise to talk to the same audiences regularly in different ways, and will always be on the look-out for new speakers who will attract paying customers. (They may even need someone to come in as an understudy for the event which has already been organized. Speakers do sometimes fall ill or have to go on business trips at the last minute and replacements have to be found – so make sure they know where to find you in such an emergency.)

Check the forthcoming events pages of trade papers, and contact the organizers. It is also worth contacting known speakers in similar fields – they may need guest presenters to fill in for them from time to time.

Contact all the associations, institutes and training organizations in your field and find out who is in charge of conferences and seminars. They will have a constant need for new blood and should know that you are in the market.

Once you have a list of potential targets, write to them regularly to up-date them on what you are doing. If you have an article published, send them a copy, with a covering letter explaining why the subject of the article would also make a useful speech.

When you get an engagement to speak, ask the organizers if you can invite a few guests of your own. If they say yes, then invite other organizers from your hit-list to come and hear you talk. Just as a struggling young actor gets agents and producers to come to see them when they are 'off-Broadway', you need to convince the right people that you are a reliable and competent speaker.

Getting your act together

You may only need to speak for a quarter of an hour, or you may need to do a whole hour or even half a day. Always make sure that you have enough material to talk for the whole of the time if necessary, and then try to encourage the audience to talk to you. Audience participation can really liven up an event (as long as one or two of them are not allowed to monopolize the time), and helps you to conserve your own energy and material.

Having a written script for the occasion gives you something to fall back on, something to show the organizers, and something to show any media which are covering the event. It also helps you to clarify your own thoughts while writing it, and to rehearse some of the key points and arguments before confronting the audience. Once the script is written, however, you should be flexible about whether you stick to it (unless the organizers want you to deliver it exactly as written for some reason). A pre-prepared essay *can* make for a very dull speech indeed, and it's worth remembering that top speakers rarely use scripts, preferring to think on their feet and respond to questions from the audience.

Getting the audience to ask questions is also a useful way of ascertaining the most important problems of the market-place. If, for example, you are an accountant and all the questions seem to be about how to cut fixed overheads, you can then prepare another talk or an article specifically on that subject, knowing that there will be people wanting to read or listen. In the early stages, at least, you should be listening as much as talking if you want to build your own knowledge base and increase your reputation. If you become arrogant and didactic too early in your career, you will alienate your audiences and find that requests for you to talk dwindle rapidly.

Provided your audiences are different, there is no reason why you can't deliver the same talk more than once, or have one basic script which evolves with changes in the market-place. You are, after all, working as a teacher in this situation, and most teachers spend a great deal of their time teaching the same subject over and over again to different pupils. Sending organizers a script will help convince them of your ability, and provided they don't think any of their customers will have heard you say the same things already, they won't mind if it has already been tried and tested on other audiences.

You may or may not be paid for such engagements. As with the articles for the trade media, it will depend on whether you approached them or they approached you. If you have been begging organizers to try you out, it might be unwise to send them an invoice when they finally agree to do so (although many of them will volunteer a fee or at least send a case of wine as a thank you). If, on the other hand, they approach you to give a talk, you can quote a daily rate. James Martin gets around $25,000 – you may have to start a little lower than that, but it will still be more than most people earn for a day's work.

If you are speaking as a representative of your employers, you may have to work out with them who should get whatever fees are involved. Most enlightened employers will let you keep any money you earn this way (unless they think your speaking engagements cause you to neglect your job), but it is always better to find out where you stand at the start.

Running your own show
In 1983 John Fenton decided to create the 'Year for Selling'. He was already well-known as a trainer and motivator in the world of selling, but he wanted to raise awareness of what he did even further. He embarked on a nationwide tour of cinemas, theatres and town halls, culminating in a series of performances at the Royal Albert Hall. Although Henry Cooper, amongst other contributors, was hired to do a half-hour spot before Fenton arrived, it is Fenton's name which is remembered by anyone who was around at the time and aware of the publicity build-up.

It was the fulfilment of a dream for Fenton, an unashamed egotist and showman, who had always wanted to stand in the centre of the Albert Hall, with all those eyes upon him. It was an ambition that came at a price: by the end of the year he had incurred losses of £80,000, but he had achieved what he set out to do. He had plenty of critics, particularly within his own industry, but no-one could ignore him any more. There wasn't anyone in marketing or selling who didn't at least know who he was, and most of them had been to one of his events, if only to see what the fuss was all about.

That £80,000 was an investment in a longer-term plan, a career-plan which led to Fenton selling his business interests for a cool £10 million in 1989, and retiring for a while to Marbella.

Not everyone has the nerve and speaking ability of John Fenton, but there are many people who have managed to build businesses on speaking and have used the resulting publicity and business opportunities to create something bigger and better than would otherwise have been possible.

Organizing seminars can simply be a marketing exercise designed to reach specific target markets. It can also provide you with an opportunity to market yourself – any costs of which will eventually be repaid by your success. If, like James Martin, you have managed to corner a sector of the market that everyone wants to learn about, you will be able to reap huge profits from any event that you are part of. If, on the other hand, you are using the seminar as a vehicle for becoming well-known, and are operating in a competitive environment (say, as a management consultant arranging general management seminars), you might have to accept the investment of some of your own money in the beginning. You may have to price the tickets a little too low in order to attract enough people, or spend more on advertising than can be recouped from ticket sales.

You should, of course, assess whether the likely losses are worth shouldering as part of a bigger, wider and more long-term plan to become well-known. Suppose, for instance, you are likely to incur losses of £10,000 on an event – you could easily have spent that much on a traditional advertising or direct mail campaign. Which would have been most effective? Does the publicity you received during the loss-making seminar mean that you will be able to increase your fee for speaking at other people's events? If, for instance, you were previously charging £500 a day, and the publicity from your own event means that you are able to double that, it will not take long to recoup the £10,000. There are also other potential spin-offs, like books, videos and audio-cassettes, which we will go into in more detail in later chapters.

Remember the first priority is to get the ball rolling – provided you don't bankrupt yourself in the process – not to make profits.

If you are putting a lot of effort into a seminar, you may be reluctant to share the limelight with anyone else. This may be a mistake. James Martin and John Fenton are both the undisputed stars of their own roadshows, but both employ guest speakers, or support acts, to help them get through the show. You might decide that it would be more fitting to make yourself a minor attraction in a show full of larger stars, giving yourself credit by association with people further up the ladder than yourself. You can do this most easily by taking guest spots in other people's seminars, but you could also take the initiative and organize them yourself, inviting the stars of your industry to speak.

You must also decide whether you and your colleagues want to handle all the administration yourselves, or whether you want to employ a professional organizer. There are companies who specialize in organizing seminars, taking care of all the administrative details, like booking conference facilities and hotel rooms (a job which needs to be done at least a year in advance if the seminar is going to be of any size and the venue is going to be in a city centre), advertising and promoting the event and making the actual arrangements on the day or week. Do you, for instance, want to get involved with the details of lunch menus and loudspeaker systems, or would you rather concentrate your energies on the content and delivery of your show?

DEVELOPING YOUR SPEAKING TALENT

Seminar organizers are always on the look-out for new talent, and are often willing to help in the early stages by providing some counselling if a speaker is particularly inexperienced or nervous, as well as help with speaker aids like audio-visual slides. On the whole, however, they expect their performers to learn from the experience of speaking, and from the feedback which comes from the audience. Every speaker has their own idiosyncracies when they talk, but if what they have to say has quality it will show through.

The fact that we have started to talk about large sums of money (few individuals could contemplate making a loss of £80,000 now, let alone in 1983) doesn't mean that anyone needs to rule themselves out of the race at this stage. You can travel as fast or as slowly as you like.

If you are running a company with a marketing budget which can afford to invest in a planned series of promotional seminars, then you can start thinking in those sort of figures. If not, then keep things small, perhaps organizing one-day seminars in a local hotel for a dozen people. Once you have done a few, you may feel confident enough to move on to something bigger, or you may decide to put yourself in the hands of a professional organizer, who will take all the financial risks and merely give you a percentage of the profits, or a fee.

MATERIAL – ORIGINATION OR REGURGITATION?

There are very few really original thinkers. For the rest of us it is a question of working with the information and knowledge which is already available and accepted, and trying to make greater sense of it by moving it about and putting it into different combinations.

Most of the people who become known as 'gurus' or 'experts' on the seminar and conference circuits are actually just very good communicators. They are skilled at finding the right information, and at explaining it to people who know nothing about it at all.

It is no coincidence that many of the most successful speakers on the seminar circuit are ex-journalists or authors. That is because writers have become adept at researching and organizing information and then presenting it to others.

Just as a schoolteacher will take text books and other sources of information, and explain and translate them for children, the good business speaker is able to understand what information it is that the audience most wants and needs to know, and knows where to find the answers.

Whatever information you need, your first call should be on the people already working in that field. When an editor takes over a magazine for the grocery industry, the chances are that he or she will know nothing about the industry when first arriving in the job. The editor might have come from another magazine for local sanitary inspectors, yet before long will know everything that is going on in the grocery industry because he or she is constantly talking to the most important people in it, and reading about what is going on. If the editor is good at communicating, he or she could soon be as well-known within that industry as the chairmen and chief executives of the biggest and most powerful supermarket chains and food manufacturers.

Another fruitful source of information are consultants, because they are constantly working on other people's problems, gaining an insight into what is happening all over their chosen industry and being able to recognize trends. If every car company in the world is doing research into an electric engine, they will be guarding everything they do with strict rules of secrecy. Consultants, however, who know all there is to know about electric engines are likely to be working with at least some of these companies, and friendly with other consultants who are working with others. It's a fair guess that those consultants are going to know more about the subject than anyone else in the world, having a broader vision of the subject than even the car companies themselves. Provided they are not too indiscreet about what is going on behind closed doors, those consultants are going to be able to earn a good living on the lecture circuit, talking about the possible future of the electric car. They have the broadest picture available to you.

Suppose, for instance, that none of the salespeople in a particular company seemed able to close a sale. Perhaps they were good at finding new leads and developing them, but unable to actually get the prospects to sign on the dotted line, and as a result the company's cashflow was suffering. A sales consultant would be able to see how the problem had originated and would draw up a plan to show how to solve it. Every sales manager in the world is going to want to know how to get more sales closed and is likely to be willing to send members of a sales team to a seminar on the topic if the speaker looks like someone with genuine, hands-on experience of the problems. So the consultant would organize a seminar to fit the problem: he or she would have both material and a ready audience to hand.

Most industries have newsletters which are packed with up-to-date information, as well as traditional trade publications. If you know what it is that the audience wants to hear, you can set out to satisfy them. If you are a cement manufacturer and you know that the one thing all builders need to know is how to save money when building house foundations, simply read all the available material on cement technology and construction techniques and apply what you learn to solving that one particular problem – you immediately have a marketable subject.

You might also apply the disciplines of one subject to another. The works of most philosophers can be adapted to fit most industries: the writings of Machiavelli and the thoughts of Attila the Hun have both been used recently as bases for management theory books. It takes imagination and lateral thinking to excel in this area, but if you have got this far, you now have the opportunity to go for the very big time.

TRAINERS AND TEACHERS

In 1969 James Martin published a book which described the rise of technology in the 1970s and 1980s with remarkable accuracy. It predicted that electronic technology would enable the best teachers to earn more than the best film stars. While few people have been able to make his prophesy come perfectly true, the trend he described is firmly in place.

Most of the techniques for self-promotion discussed in this chapter are inextricably linked with the business of teaching and training. People come to hear speakers because they want to learn something. They may have a problem and be searching for a solution, or they may simply have heard that this person can show them a way of improving their lives in some way. As soon as you stand up on a stage and start talking, you have put yourself in the position of a teacher, and while the people that make a profession out of teaching our children become less and less well paid, those who can provide specialist groups of adults with the education that they want will become better and better rewarded.

In many cases, people who become established as good speakers end up developing training facilities within their own companies. If, for instance, you are running a marketing company and you become known on the speaking circuit for your expertise in the database marketing field, you will be attracting audiences who have problems in that area. If the people in the audience like what you say, they are going to want to know more, which means they are probably going to want someone to train their marketing people in the subject. They might simply tell everyone in their company to come and see you on stage. Alternatively, they might ask you to come in to train their people in-house.

The question you have to ask yourself if you become a successful speaker is, 'Do I want to go into the training business?' If you are already successful as a pundit on your subject, do you want to expend time and energy on running courses on the subject for managers, when you could be concentrating on running the advertising agency which you founded yourself and are working hard to promote?

You will have to decide for yourself where to draw the line: it will usually become a matter of financial priorities and personal tastes. Some people find that they love teaching others; some find it is fun to stand up and talk for an hour or two, but then soon become bored. The important thing is to be aware of the opportunities which teaching and training can provide for developing a reputation, and to exploit them as fully as possible.

If you are just starting out in your chosen career, part-time teaching could be a useful way to develop communication skills, and to clarify your thoughts about your own abilities and the structure of your profession. It can also be a useful extra source of income at a time when money is usually tight.

Most colleges welcome offers of help from people who are already practising a profession. If, for instance, you are working in an advertising agency, you might well be able to teach students on marketing courses. If you are a practising accountant, you might be able to lecture on general business studies courses at a local polytechnic or a privately-run business school. Write to likely colleges telling them your qualifications and letting them know of your willingness to give up a few evenings a week. The more experience you have at explaining yourself and your profession to others, the better equipped you will be for the big time.

GETTING YOUR SPEECH COVERED

Whenever you speak in public, always make sure that the relevant press know about it. As soon as you know that you are going to be appearing somewhere, send a press release announcing the fact to your trade papers, with a picture. If they publish it, you might improve the attendance of the seminar at the same time as letting people know that you are now an acknowledged expert in your subject area.

When writing the script for your speech, try to build in some controversial statement, prediction or angle which you will be able to pull out and turn into a news story. If, for instance, you are talking about 'developments in car engines', you might predict that within 20 years all road vehicles will be completely silent and pollution-free. You could go on to illustrate the implications of this for people living near roads which are currently noisy, and for road safety.

Of course, you must be able to support such statements with at least some statistics or evidence of serious thought. But there is nearly always a controversial way of phrasing everything (just look at the way tabloid newspapers can create shocking headlines for the most mundane of news stories); the trick is to catch the attention of editors as well as readers and listeners.

When you know what your theme is going to be, write to each of the editors on your hit-list, giving them an outline of what the speech is going to be about and asking if they would like an article based on it, or if they would like to meet you to talk about it. Check that the organizers of the seminar are happy for you to do this, and that you are not duplicating their efforts or giving away too much ahead of time.

Alternatively, you could ask editors if they would like to see the final manuscript, with a view to publishing part or all of it after the event (you must be certain in this case that you are going to stick exactly to your script). Make sure they are all aware of the controversial angle which you are taking. The seminar organizers will probably invite the most important media to attend, but you should check that all the best people on your hit-list are included. If they aren't and you don't want to contact them yourself, ask the publicity department of the organizing company if their names can be added.

Provide the organizers with a full curriculum vitae and photographs of yourself, which their publicity people can circulate and use for their own promotional material. If what you have to say is *extremely* controversial, it might be better to wait until the day of the talk before approaching the media – then circulate the press release as a hot news story. Be sure, however, to consider publication deadlines when doing this.

If the angle you are taking is very newsworthy, you might have to ask for the organizers' help in arranging a news conference after the event to answer any questions which your words may have given rise to. In any event you should make sure that you meet any journalists who have taken the trouble to turn up to listen to you. If they have bothered to turn up, they are probably planning to write something, and the longer they spend talking to you, the more often you are likely to be quoted in whatever they write. Make sure that you have some spare copies of your manuscript to give to them in case they haven't received one, or have mislaid it.

Giving a talk is always an opportunity for gaining media coverage and for increasing your profile. Don't waste it.

CHAPTER FIVE

On to the Airwaves

SO NOW YOU are a confident and experienced speaker, who knows your subject inside out. If there are questions which you don't know the answer to, you are quite happy to admit it, because you are still confident that you are as good as you should be for the position you are assuming – that of an expert in your field.

You have also had enough practice speaking to live audiences to know that you can talk fluently and intelligently on most aspects of your subject. Like the actor who starts in the repertory company, displaying his skills to a local audience, you must now look for wider showcases for your talents. Next stop will probably be the world of radio and tapes.

Anyone who is out of the habit of listening to the radio could easily underestimate its importance to certain segments of the market. People stuck at home, like the elderly or housewives with young children, listen to it a great deal, as do teenagers and people like lorry drivers who spend a lot of time on the road. During the last war, and in the 15 years after that, it was the nation's major source of canned entertainment and information. The arrival of television pushed it from being the most powerful medium for widespread communication into an equal second with the printed media; but it is still powerful. Since then there has been a proliferation of small stations serving local markets. These underpin the original broadcasting giants which continue much as they always have, or so it seems to the casual listener.

There are still large audiences to be won by some programmes, and radio has the advantage for the beginner of being an altogether gentler and less frightening introduction to the electronic media than the all-encompassing world of television.

There are specialist programmes, and there are general discussion programmes which look at the news and need people to discuss its implications in some detail. There is a radio equivalent to almost every type of printed medium, and there is probably a national and local version of each of them if you have the time to search them out.

STARTING LOCAL

Most local radio stations have limited finances and are therefore glad of any genuine offers of help from people who can contribute something to their listeners.

The first rule is to listen to the stations concerned and become familiar with their output. Some, of course, are purely interested in popular music, but others may take up particular local causes or interests. Just as with the local press, there are openings for experts in all fields.

There are three ways in which you could be called upon to contribute: talking 'live' in the studio; via a taped interview with a reporter; or over the telephone.

The advantage of going live is that no-one can edit your words to sound like something you didn't mean to say. The disadvantage is that you can't correct mistakes or eradicate stammerings.

Once you have familiarized yourself with the contents of the station, find out who produces the programmes which you are interested in, and write to them with a short synopsis of your idea, offering to meet them to discuss it in more detail, or to prepare a draft script for a pilot programme which they could consider.

If you haven't had a reply within a couple of weeks, telephone to ask if they have received the material and whether it is likely to be of use. If they show a glimmer of interest, try to get in to meet them, so that they can see that you are keen and serious, and that you have the ability to handle the project.

Make sure that all relevant producers have your telephone number, and send them a steady stream of opinions on your subject which are newsworthy. If, for instance, you are an expert on Eastern European affairs, it would have been a good idea to let as many media people as possible know that you existed during the period of revolution in that part of the world.

GOING NATIONAL

If you really want to cast the net wide, you can approach all the local independent and BBC stations simultaneously. One way round the geographical problems of this approach is to record an interview with one of the syndicating companies, and have it distributed to all the stations. If your topic is really newsworthy, they will arrange for this to be done at their expense; if you are merely hoping to jump on to a bandwagon, you may have to pay to have the tape made and distributed. If you have to pay, be very sure that you are making a genuine contribution to the subject: stations will not play tapes which are obviously puffs for the speaker or the speaker's company, nor anything boring or waffly.

If you are ready to talk to national radio stations, you can apply the same principles as the local ones (bearing in mind, of course, that what appeals to your local community may not appeal to listeners nationwide). Listen to the programmes and find out who the producers are, then send them ideas for features or for whole programmes. Send them copies of articles which you have written, to show that you are already something of an expert, and make sure that they have your telephone number to hand should they ever need to contact you. It might also be worth sending round a short sample tape of yourself talking on your subject, so that they can hear your speaking voice.

GOING INTERNATIONAL

Once you become known as a useful source of information and chat, you will find that the producers approach you rather than the other way round. You will also find that your contributions find their way all round the world, mainly through the BBC World Service Network.

The drawback of radio is that there is little you can do to prolong the life of your appearances. Once the show is over it is almost immediately forgotten. If you appear regularly enough, your name might start to be remembered, and it will probably be remembered by other people in your particular field of endeavour; a one-off appearance, however, will not normally make much impact as far as your reputation is concerned. It does, nevertheless, give you one more marketing tool for your long-term strategy.

Always tape your broadcasts for your own records, and send copies to other producers to demonstrate that you are experienced in broadcasting and able to handle live interviews, phone-ins or whatever it is that you have been called on to do. Always enclose a covering letter explaining who you are and why you are sending them. Recordings might also be useful to send to television producers at the next stage of your campaign. Never send your master tapes, and don't expect to have the copies you send out returned. Have transcripts made of the tapes, so that you can study your own words and work on ways to improve the sense of what you were saying, and your delivery.

You may also be able to adapt transcripts into articles for relevant magazines. Let the editor know that your words have been broadcast. This should add extra weight to them – provided they are still topical.

GETTING TAPED

The audio cassette is mostly linked to the teaching and training aspects of self-promotion which we began talking about in the last chapter.

If your words are worthy of radio broadcasting, and if people are willing to pay money or spend valuable time coming to hear you talk at seminars and conferences, there may be a market for tapes of your work. Sold on the same basis as books, they are normally aimed at the same market as seminars, but are usually cheaper than tickets and almost certainly more convenient to listen to. Experts in sales and in diet and exercise regimes sell a lot of cassettes, and some tapes are distributed to special interest groups in the same way as printed newsletters (this also applies, on a potentially much larger scale, to video tapes, as we will discuss in the next chapter).

As with the tapes for local radio, however, you are going to have to be prepared to invest money at this stage. As well as the costs of making and distributing the tapes, there will also be packaging and marketing costs, which may or may not be recoverable. Once you have committed yourself to this sort of expenditure, you have definitely nailed your colours to the mast. No-one will be in any doubt that you intend to be very famous indeed!

CHAPTER SIX

The Power of the Small Screen

TELEVISION CAN ELEVATE people of seemingly limited talents to super-star status, and yet totally ignore some of the most important and powerful people in society. Or perhaps those people are choosing to ignore the medium.

In the past it was a very exclusive club; a small world which did not welcome intrusion from the outside. The same faces kept appearing on the same channels. First there was only one channel in Britain, and it took four decades for the number to rise to four.

In the 1990s, however, we are going to see that all change. We have already become used to video recorders in our homes and treat them as casually as our familiar old kitchen appliances. In the business world it is now as common to be given a corporate video to look at as a brochure or annual report. The use of video will continue to spread as the cost of making your own programmes continues to drop. We are not yet watching either cable or satellite television in any great numbers, but then it took us a while to get used to the idea of break-fast and day-time television as well.

As with the printed media, we are seeing a proliferation of new television outlets. None of us have time to watch them all, so the market is becoming more competitive. In order to attract our atten-tion, as well as the money of advertisers, programme makers and distributors are becoming far more targeted and specialized in what they produce. National stations are still pumping out material which is the visual equivalent of the tabloid and other daily newspapers – full of game shows, chat shows, pop music, cartoons, drama, news and wide-interest documentaries – but more narrowly targeted methods of distribution are growing stronger, catering for very specialized tastes and making the national channels begin to look like dinosaurs.

Some of them will, like tabloid newspapers, head for the bottom of the market, becoming supermarkets of fun and light entertain-ment for the mass markets; others may gravitate upwards to cater for the more affluent and discerning viewers, but they will find them-selves competing against increasingly sophisticated new methods of distribution.

You can already buy videos on almost any subject you like. They might be dramatized documentaries about Gerard Manley Hopkins, or programmes teaching you how to wind-surf, with novices being taught by a former champion (both real examples produced by the Picture Publishing Company). They might be business training films, or the products of educational establishments like the Open University.

Suddenly the very best teachers, experts and speakers are available to everyone. Imagine what that makes possible. The very best lecturers at the very best universities can only speak to a limited number of people in a classroom. Anyone else wanting to share their thoughts has to read their books – a cold, arms-length method of learning. But what if you could get hold of videos of these lecturers in action? Imagine what that would have meant in the past: you could have heard Charles Darwin or Bertrand Russell explaining – first-hand – their beliefs and theories; you could have attended art master-classes with Picasso or listened to Dickens talking about popular writing. Whatever your profession or interests there are going to be people you long to meet and learn from, and may never get near in the flesh, but whom video could bring to you.

If you are a manager and you want to hear the words of Tom Peters, do you wait until he is next touring in your country and spend £500 per head to hear him for a day? Or do you rent one of his videos for two days at a cost of £145? You could learn to play tennis from Boris Becker and mathematics from Stephen Hawking, take legal advice from a top QC and cookery classes from Raymond Blanc – all via video.

Many companies are already setting up their own internal television networks, allowing senior management to broadcast direct to the whole workforce. People who might work for a giant company for 30 years and never set eyes on the chairman and senior executives, can see and hear them every week or every day if necessary. They can be immediately informed of boardroom decisions and changes in direction. In some cases, they can answer back and ask questions on interactive satellite links.

Soon we will all be as used to appearing on television, or talking to people on the screen, as we are to using the telephone. Newsreaders and chat show hosts are already getting us used to the idea of talking to someone on a screen or monitor from a studio; businesses are already using video conferencing to hold international meetings without leaving their home towns, or in some cases without even leaving their offices.

It is a revolution just as great as the invention of printing all those centuries ago. Suddenly we can all communicate with carefully chosen audiences in a hundred different ways, but only some people will know how to exploit these changes effectively, how to use the opportunities to become famous.

THE TRADITIONAL OUTLETS

The major – or 'dinosaur' – channels are still by far the most powerful medium available, and will continue to be so for at least another decade, just at *The Times* continued to be the most powerful newspaper in the land for many years after other papers appeared to rival it. Eventually, however, it became just one more quality newspaper among many, but still a useful medium to appear in. So what are the options for publicity offered by the major channels and their programme makers?

GETTING ON THE NEWS

Unless you are actually making news yourself – in which case the chances are you will already have a considerable publicity machine working on your behalf or will be desperately trying to avoid prying cameras – the only opportunity for appearing is as an expert 'commentator'.

Politicians are particularly adept at this, although they are seldom actually experts in the subjects they are pontificating on, merely the mouthpieces of invisible experts within the civil service and in their own parties. If there is a major motorway crash, there is quite likely to be a government politician taking the opportunity to talk about the problems of drinking and driving, and someone from the opposition accusing the government of not spending enough money on road improvement.

The only reason television companies have to continually resort to these people for comment is because they know where to find them, and they know that they will always have something to say. Well-known politicians are consummate experts in self-hype: they know exactly how to get the cameras pointing at them at every opportunity.

If you are a genuine expert on the design of motorways, or you have made a life-time's study of the statistics of road deaths, it is you they should be talking to, and it is up to *you* to make sure they know who you are.

If you have done the groundwork discussed in earlier chapters, you will already have a portfolio of articles you have written for magazines and newspapers, and will be used to talking on platforms and on the radio. Now is the time to send copies of the articles to all the producers of television news programmes, telling them who you are and giving them your phone number.

Have a list of relevant telephone numbers prepared, so that if a major news story in your field breaks, you can ring all the relevant people to let them know that you have theories and opinions on what has happened. It might be that you know a lot about a particular country where a major story breaks, or you might be an expert in human behaviour and be able to comment on soccer hooliganism. If you are a lawyer, you could discuss eccentric sentences passed by judges; if you are an accountant, you could give an insight into a major corporate fraud which might just have come to light; and a stockbroking analyst can discuss why a company has gone into liquidation.

Once you have become known as a good talker and source of material, you will find national channels ringing you up at all hours with requests. Some experts find that on the day a major news story breaks, they spend most of their time in studio cars being whisked from breakfast television to a morning radio show to a lunch-time news broadcast, and on to record some major pieces for the evening. As you become more well-known you can begin to demand that they send their camera crews to you, which will save you time, and also add to your apparent status as a guru on your subject.

From news commentary you can move on to studio discussion and current affairs programmes, either about specific stories or generic issues. There might be a programme about air safety following a rash of air crashes. If you are an expert in aircraft design, you might be asked to take part in a programme with an airline chief, a consumer group spokesperson on air safety and someone who has been personally involved in an air crash. It is hard to know when these programmes are being planned and by whom, so all you can do is ensure that as many producers as possible know who you are and where to contact you when the need arises.

TRAINING

The amount of money earned by the ex-disc jockeys and journalists who manage to become household names through their television appearances is shocking to many people. Do they, you might ask yourself, really merit such enormous sums? All they have to do is chat away in front of the cameras, meet interesting people and open the occasional supermarket.

The first time you find yourself in front of the cameras, you might find yourself being much more sympathetic to their cause. Even the most confident people find the cold eye of the camera – not to mention blank expressions of the crew manning the cameras, sound equipment, lighting and ancillary machinery – leaves them perspiring, tongue-tied wrecks. You suddenly become aware of nervous twitches you never realized you had, and in trying to instantly eradicate them you are unable to think what it is you are supposed to be talking about.

Of course, things improve with practice: archive recordings of familiar television personalities of today usually show that they weren't always as relaxed and confident as they now appear. They have had to learn and polish their craft like anyone else.

The question is, can you afford the time to get the necessary experience? If you are invited to a studio to talk on your subject, it is probably a break you have been working towards for years. Can you afford to mess it up? If you prove to be a complete dead loss in front of the camera, the chances are you will be edited out of the programme and never asked to participate in another, at least not by anyone who has witnessed your first débâcle.

Some people are naturals when the camera is turned on them, but not many. Most of us need to learn some techniques and get some practice in using machines such as auto-cues. Many large companies now take the precaution of training their managers in television techniques as part of their public relations and crisis-management programmes. Others provide training for appearances in corporate videos. Take whatever training is being offered by your company. If it isn't being offered, then ask for it. If they decline and you think there is a real chance you will be able to get yourself in front of the cameras, invest in some sort of training yourself, even if it is only from a local drama coach.

If you don't manage to get any formal training, make sure that you are very clear in your mind what is expected of you. Watch a lot of television speakers and observe how they behave when the cameras are on them. How do they sit? Do they use their hands when talking? Do they talk loudly or softly? Do they smile? - all the questions you asked yourself when you started appearing on platforms.

Many of the same lessons that applied to your stage appearances will apply under studio conditions. The most important trick to learn is to appear relaxed, either by truly managing to make yourself so, or by controlling your fears and making them work for you in a positive way, giving an aggression and authority to your words. Think about the effect you want to have on the viewers, and then practise in front of the mirror, or in front of a video camera, until you are happy with your own performance.

Don't worry about fluffs and mistakes. A small stutter on a word may sound terrible inside your head, but don't become so obsessed by the slip-up that you lose the drift of what you are saying. The chances are that the viewer hasn't even noticed the mistake. We all stutter and stammer on some words when we talk: we all say 'er' and 'um' occasionally. If we didn't, we would sound as if we were reading a script instead of talking naturally. When you see your first performance played back, you will be amazed at how small the gestures and expressions which you were so self-conscious about actually appear. If you have a bigger speech problem of any sort, you will either need strong nerves and the ability to brazen it out (look how many successful presenters, performers and politicians have lisps, stutters and stammers), or take some professional speech therapy advice.

GETTING YOUR OWN SHOW

It sounds like an impossibility, but why should it be? Just look at the enormous range of people who have had shows of their own, or even a series, and then gone on to become permanent fixtures on the screen, ending up as celebrities on panel games and raw material for impersonators: astrologers and astronomers, gardening and keep-fit experts, cooks and wine connoisseurs, architects and art historians, naturalists and sportspeople, antiques experts and travel writers, journalists and weathermen, doctors and psychologists, child-care experts and agony aunts, professors and vets, hairdressers and make-up artists, old soldiers and solicitors, DIY experts and dress designers, farmers and dog handlers. The list is endless.

If you are a good performer and can make your subject relevant and interesting to the viewing public, you could end up with a show of your own. You just have to make sure that the producers know about you and appreciate your skills.

So let's assume that you have established your credibility through your writings and public appearances. You may also have been on the occasional current affairs programme or chat show. The next step is to become either one of the presenters or a 'guest spot' in someone else's show.

Anyone who writes on a particular subject should be able to find an equivalent slot on television which they could compete for. Travel writers are a good example, as are political and financial commentators. Agony aunts are greatly appreciated by producers because their material is such compulsive viewing and because they usually like the sound of their own voices.

Once you are within the environment of the television studio you can start to make an impression. The first thing is to excel at the job you are asked to do. Ensure that you have interesting things to say and that you deliver them well. Do your research and preparation work thoroughly before you arrive on set, so that you acquire a reputation for being reliable and professional. Spend time socializing with producers and directors, letting them know that you are keen to do more, and that you are full of ideas for new shows.

If you are there to do a cookery spot and you get on well with a producer, you could suggest a series looking at the cuisine of different countries, or talking to different famous chefs. The ideas don't have to be original, but the producers have to be convinced that you would be able to make the programmes watchable. Don't be afraid of your ideas being seen as eccentric – who would have believed that a series about sheepdogs and their owners rounding up sheep would be one of the most popular programmes on television?

How successful you are at this stage will depend a great deal on your personality. There are almost certainly many people who can cook as well as Keith Floyd, but can they catch the public's imagination in the same way? There are many astrologers who give more detailed and serious advice than Russell Grant, but are they such skilled showmen? Through the years there have been many names which have become synonymous with their subjects because of their television appearances, not because of their pre-eminence in their field: Fanny Craddock in cookery, Barry Bucknell in DIY, Percy Thrower in gardening, David Frost as an international business tycoon, Derek Jameson as a Fleet Street editor. All of them appealed to the public in some way (although that appeal can extend to them being people the public 'loves to hate').

If you don't manage to convince any of the people you talk to that you should have your own show, don't give up. Go away and think up more detailed ideas and put together proposals. The more detailed they are the more likely you are to get the interest of the people with the money. Write them up like marketing reports, explaining what the format of the programmes would be, who they would appeal to, how they would be made, why they would be cheap/easy to make, and any other facts which are likely to make the project attractive. Give the producers enough material to convince them that it would fill a whole hour, or would make a series.

It might be a course of educational programmes on how to plumb a house; or a series of programmes on how to choose and train a pony; or a series on how to invest money or start a business; or how to get divorced; or ways in which technology will effect our lives in the next ten years. It doesn't matter what the subject is, as long as it is something which you know a lot about and can sell convincingly, *and as long as you will be the central character in the show or series.* Don't forget that our primary objective is to make you famous, not to make you a television writer.

WORKING BEHIND THE SCREEN

You may get taken on as an adviser to a series, or as a script consultant, or any number of other functions which will not help in getting your face and name any better known to the general public, although it will help with your curriculum vitae as you continue to move upwards. If those sorts of job are offered, it is certainly worth taking them if you have the time, since it gives you further opportunities to get to know directors, producers and other writers

– all of whom might be able to turn you into a star if you can enthuse them enough with your personality and your ideas.

Don't limit yourself to the people you know at one station: go to all of them and constantly be making new contacts. Television is a fast-moving business and there are always bright young people coming up who are looking for an idea which will help them to get on the next rung. You have to search them out and get to know them wherever they are.

INDEPENDENT PRODUCERS

The changes in the structure of broadcasting in Britain during the 1980s mean that many programmes are not made by the BBC or ITV companies themselves, but are bought in from independent production houses.

This is still a very young market and it is hard to find out who is doing what and when, but there are a vast number of producers and directors looking for projects which they can make in conjunction with the major channels, or which they will be able to afford to make for themselves and then sell. Because it is an immature market-place, it is relatively easy to set up in business, and even easier to go out again. The result is that any list of companies that you might be able to get hold of will be inconclusive and almost immediately out of date.

Again, you need to meet and talk to as many of the relevant people as possible. This is time-consuming, and if you have got to this stage, you are probably beginning to treat the performing side of your career as a job in itself. It might be worth hiring somebody else, like an assistant or a secretary, to spend a day or two a week finding out the names of producers and writing to them suggesting your ideas and sending synopses.

If an independent producer makes a programme with you, the chances are that the final product is going to be appearing some-where, because the producer will want to get his or her money back. So even if the producer does not manage to sell to one of the major networks, he or she is going to be looking for other ways to recoup costs. It will help you to win the producer's confidence at the begin-ning if you can demonstrate that you have thought the problems through and can suggest alternative ways in which the producer could distribute the programmes.

VIDEO MAGAZINES

Video magazines are a new industry and are still finding their feet. The principle is the same as any ordinary specialist magazine. You define a target market and then put together a video programme with news and features on the industry concerned, and persuade people to advertise in it, or subscribe to it or, if possible, both. The reason that the industry is still at the fledgling stage is because of the high costs involved in making the programmes and the relative inaccessibility of video. Readers can pick up and flick through a magazine anywhere – on the train, on the lavatory – but with a video, viewers have to make time to sit down in front of the television, time which they might prefer to spend with their families or doing something else.

If, however, the content of the magazine is so interesting to you that you are willing to pay to receive it, you will certainly sit down and watch it. One of the first users of the medium was the sex industry, and they had no trouble persuading their subscribers to watch, although even they have run into financial difficulties at times.

Keep-fit and other hobby subjects have also done well (led by Jane Fonda and her workouts), and now professional subjects are beginning to establish themselves. A news and features programme for information systems managers, for instance, might not sound exciting, but if you are an information systems manager there is probably no other television programme catering specifically for you. If the marketing material which accompanies the package can convince you that the material inside will be of use to you in your job, you will probably buy it.

If you can think of a unique selling point which will make your programme idea compulsive viewing for a particular target market, you could be in business. You will also have to have a lot of ideas on how to keep overheads down. It will not be practical to send camera teams all over the world to get news footage, for instance. You will need to base as much of the programme as possible in the studio, and make use of public relations material which other people will be happy to give you. It will also be helpful if you can suggest a sponsoring company or other sources of finance to the producer.

Training and education videos

The training market is one where video has become firmly entrenched. John Cleese, who sold his interests in Video Arts Ltd at the end of the 1980s for a reported £10 million, is often cited as the man who made it all possible, and his witty films on customer care and other marketing and business skills have certainly done a great deal to alert the market-place to the value of video as a training tool.

It is a medium which nearly all business gurus are involved with. If your ideas are good enough, and you are a compulsive enough performer, there is really no limit to the number of business areas which video will work in.

SATELLITE AND CABLE CHANNELS

These have been slow to establish themselves, but they are beginning to appear. There is a channel which talks to doctors early in the morning, and in America there are several which cater for particular industries, such as the computer industry. Like video magazines, they have to ensure that their material is of direct relevance to the viewer, which means it must either have news significance – e.g. a technical breakthrough which will change the way things are done, or a new product launch which competitors will need to know about – or it will need to be educational in some way.

Selling your programmes to these specialized channels can help to recover the costs of production and can also provide a well-targeted platform for you to talk from.

Once you have made a programme of any sort on video, you should send copies round to the producers on your hit-list who may not yet be aware of how well you perform in front of the camera (assuming that you do perform well). It should be accompanied by a synopsis for an idea which develops the themes instigated in the existing video. If, for instance, you are a vet and the video is a programme on vaccinating pigs, sponsored by a pharmaceutical company, you could send copies to producers, suggesting a series on healthcare for farmyard animals generally, which could be marketed to the farming and food manufacturing industries.

APPEARING IN YOUR OWN ADVERTISEMENTS

This avenue is only really open to entrepreneurs who have an advertising budget and the power to demand of their agencies that they be featured personally. For those who use it, it works well. Bernard Matthews with his turkey farms, Victor Kiam with his shavers, and others selling everything from second-hand televisions to giant American car companies, have found that they are able to create catch-phrases and characters which are instantly recognizable to their buying publics and to wider audiences.

Victor Kiam, for instance, has been able to build on his reputation as a businessman to write books and promote himself to the general business-reading public. It could be argued that he is doing this for the good of the company, that the more famous he becomes, the more products his company can sell. This justification is not watertight. Companies which are associated with one personality can have problems when that person wants to retire or slow down. They can also go on looking small long after they have grown large. The stock market, for instance, is not comfortable with companies which are associated too strongly with one person. What happens, it asks, if that person falls under a bus tomorrow?

For the personalities themselves, however, being at the head of a company with a high public profile through advertising can work wonders for their personal fame. Some, like Robert Maxwell, can grow large on the back of it if they are willing to put up with a certain amount of personal abuse and indignity, and if they are strong enough characters and good enough businesspeople.

In America the greatest exponent of this style of self-promotion has been Lee Iacocca. He first came to the attention of the general public in advertisements for Chrysler cars. The public became intrigued and wanted to know more about him. They discovered an interesting personal and business story of a hard-working Italian immigrant who had climbed to the top of the Ford company and then fell out with Henry Ford. His story was as good as any from *Dynasty* or *Dallas*. He went on to save the Chrysler company, one of the bedrocks of American capitalism – which was foundering in the face of Japanese competition – and he was held up as a national hero. A rash of books by and about him followed and at one time he was actually being thought of as a candidate for the US Presidency (no less likely than a bit-part actor making it to the White House). Iacocca is a classic example of what is possible with the right material and the right exploitation. He started by becoming expert in his subject, the motor industry. He built a reputation as an executive who got things done. Once he reached a position of eminence, he made sure that everyone within the industry was aware of what he was doing. When the opportunity arose to present himself to a wider public, he took it, and by then he had built up a personal story which everyone wanted to know about.

CASHING IN AND TYING IN

Once you are appearing regularly on television, or have a major vehicle in the form of a programme about you, or a series which you are presenting, it is time to devote yourself to some serious self-promotion.

Anyone who appears on the screen is of interest to the general public. Why this should be is a mystery, but it probably stems from the insatiable appetite for gossip among people with time on their hands. Anyone who watches a lot of television almost certainly has time on their hands, and will, therefore, be looking for something to gossip about. If you were the milkman, they would be talking about you over the fence with their neighbours, but you have come into their house from another world. The only way they are going to be able to find out more about you is through the media.

This is where some famous people – especially those who have had fame thrust upon them – begin to find it distasteful. Modest actors (there are some), who happen to land parts in very successful soap operas or comedy series, suddenly find that their private lives are splashed across the front pages of tabloid newspapers. If they haven't prepared themselves sufficiently for fame, that can be very upsetting. The media can be very judgmental and the public will more often than not follow the lead set by journalists. The hounding of Russell Harty when he was on his deathbed was a particularly good example, but virtually every pop star, actor or sports star has been subjected to it at some time. They are accused of sexual deviation, of heartlessness and meanness and everything else that anyone can be persuaded to say about them.

Stars of the business and teaching professions are no different. We will look at the problems of scandal and how to use them to your advantage in more detail in Chapter 11. At this stage we will simply recognize that the potential for turning a fleeting career on television into something more lasting is open to anyone who wants to exploit the opportunities and pay the price.

There is nearly always a gap of some months between the making of a television programme and its broadcast. During that time you need to be preparing the ground for a large-scale publicity build-up.

Television companies have very sophisticated public relations departments, and you need to make it known to these people that you are keen to co-operate in any way you can, and to put forward some ideas of your own about how you could help with the publicity. If they are putting all their weight behind your programme, you may not have to do anything else. They have the ability to get you on to chat shows and interviewed in magazines and newspapers about your programme. If, however, you are making a relatively small-budget and specialized show, you may not merit their full attention and may need to undertake some self-promotion as well.

Prepare a new hit-list of any editors and journalists whom you think might be interested in you, the programme and its contents. Remember that now you are on television you can start to be less modest and approach national and general interest publications in the same way as your own trade papers. Do not hold yourself back with false modesty now.

If you find the thought of promoting yourself too blatantly embarrassing, you can always do it at arm's length by appointing someone else as your press officer. It could be your secretary, your spouse or a friend who owns a public relations company. Anyone who can be equipped with some headed paper and a telephone number can write on your behalf, explaining what you are doing and suggesting that you would make an interesting subject for them to write about.

Your aim is to let people know that you are now sufficiently highly thought of to be given your own television show. You want to make them watch the show, and you want them to accept ideas for further ways in which you can promote yourself.

Professional television celebrities, such as actors and comedians, can turn one successful television series into an entire career. They open supermarkets, give after-dinner speeches and cabarets, write books (or have books written for them or about them), appear on quiz shows and in endless magazine profiles.

For most people that sort of full-time celebrity would not be appropriate (or desirable), but many of the mechanics which lead to it are the same for anyone wanting to build a reputation on a more serious level. Now that you are a television personality, you will find that editors are more willing to carry articles by you because your name will add credibility to their journals. They will also be more likely to want to quote your opinions in the news columns and to interview you for features.

You could suggest that you write a series of articles to accompany the television programme, or answer queries after it has appeared. You could approach other television producers and suggest ways in which they could use the interest stimulated by the programme to create discussion programmes.

The first step is to write to everyone on your hit-list and let them know that you are making the programme. This could be done in the form of a press release with a new photograph. Then follow this up with a letter asking if they would be interested in meeting for a chat, or in an article on the subject of the programme.

You can also use this as an opportunity for some direct sales promotion within your own industry. Suppose, for instance, that you are an expert in trees and are making a series on how to save old trees and plant new ones. You could prepare a letter to send to all the landowners, farmers and landscape gardeners in your area alerting them to the fact that the programme is coming and offering to come and provide some free advice (making sure that you know how to turn a speculative call into a sale of some sort). If you are a solicitor and you are getting a series of advice spots on a popular consumer programme, you could circulate this information to a thousand potential clients in your area, suggesting that they watch the programmes and, if they have any further queries, contact your office.

You could arrange a series of professional workshops or seminars, inviting people to attend (or selling them tickets if you think you can get away with it) and using the television exposure as an advertisement and reference for your abilities. It is the equivalent of the actor in a successful television series doing some local theatre work at the same time.

What you don't want to happen after all this hard work, is for the programme to be broadcast at 11pm, and for no-one to notice it has happened. It is no good in ten years' time trying to convince people that you appeared on television, if no-one can remember having seen you or having heard your name. Make sure everyone knows that it is happening at the time.

CHAPTER SEVEN

Publishing a Book

PUBLISHING A BOOK on your chosen subject can be as big a career step as appearing on television. If you do it right, it could provide you with a more long-lasting method of self-promotion and a greater degree of intellectual authority. A historian who writes a book on Cromwell is more likely to be respected by his peer group than another who presents a series of television programmes on the subject. The latter is likely to be envied and dismissed as a mere entertainer.

The same is true in any profession where there is a premium on depth of knowledge or a snobbery about the electronic media. Someone who has arrived on television can be dismissed as having had a lucky break, whereas a person who has written a book has undeniably achieved something by themselves (although they may have had a lot of help, as we will discuss in a moment), and, whether you agree with their views or not, that generally commands a certain level of respect.

Books hold a strange fascination for people who are unable to write them and who seldom read them. Perhaps it is a tradition of respect which goes back to the classroom, or perhaps it is because writing is a skill which everyone can relate to in one way or another.

Whatever it is, it works: people are invariably impressed with the news that you have written a book on your subject, even if it was some years ago. It is as if you have managed to take whatever you hold in your head and have packaged it in a form which everyone can understand and evaluate. As long as you were just pontificating on a platform or in newspaper articles you were no different from everyone else. But a book is something with a life and soul of its own, marking its creator out as something different, giving them a stamp of credibility. At school you may have assumed that everything you read in the text books was fact: it was in the book, so it must be true. That tendency to be impressed by books seems to stay with us. To write a book, the only raw material you need is your thoughts and the skills of your printers and publishers.

WHO WANTS TO READ YOU?

The question that begs answering is, who actually reads all the books which are produced? Somewhere in the region of a thousand new books a week are published in the UK, and they have to fight for attention with all that has gone before. A classic book might stay in print for 200 years; even a modestly successful business book might be around for ten or 20 years. Who on earth has the time to read one book a week, let alone a thousand?

The answer is that very few books are actually read from cover to cover by anyone outside the author's own friends and family (and even then they may not be attended to very closely). One or two books become classics in each profession at any one time, and everyone may have an attempt at reading them, although it is unknown how many people succeed in getting past the first few pages.

In the management field, for instance, *In Search of Excellence* by Tom Peters and Bob Waterman and *The One Minute Manager* by Ken Blanchard are both giant sellers. The latter is very short and can be read at one sitting – that is its unique selling point – so it has probably been more genuinely read than any other. *In Search of Excellence* is a heavy tome, which has since been joined by a number of sequels from both authors. It is full of long case histories which illustrate the authors' general theories. It would be very time-consuming to read in their entirety, yet each section would certainly be read by the companies and industries involved. Students of management would read the whole thing, as would avid readers of all business books and those hoping to write books of their own.

Beyond that small circle of certain readers, however, there are millions of people who bought the book because it was the product you were supposed to buy if you were a modern-thinker. The publicity suggested that it had valuable lessons for the reader to learn (which indeed it did), and many would have bought it with the genuine intention of studying its lessons. The book caught a trend at just the right moment and came to symbolize it. Tom Peters did not invent excellence; neither did the companies he wrote about. Excellence is a concept which has been around since the beginning of time; it was just that few people before had thought about running their businesses within that context. It was a new way of looking at things.

Many of the people who bought the book would have been able to grasp what it was about with just a casual browsing. The lesson was easily learned: they did not have to study the minute details of how each company described had achieved excellence in their particular field in order to understand the importance of the concept.

So it seems that most of the words written in books are wasted on most of the people who buy them. Yet books confer a seriousness on a subject and on the authors. They provide the status of glossy covers and nicely printed pages. They signify that the author, and the subject, are of importance and have something new to offer.

Tom Peters is a management consultant. He merely goes into

companies and observes what it is that they are doing which is working well, and reports it back. There are thousands of consultants doing equally good jobs, but because he wrote a best selling book, he is world-famous and a multi-millionaire.

Mark McCormack was already a successful entrepreneur and marketeer, but by writing *What They Don't Teach You at Harvard Business School*, he was able to demonstrate that fact to a wide audience. While purporting to show ambitious young entrepreneurs how they could become as successful as he was, he was also subtly spreading the message of his own achievements.

Many university professors and other academics use books as stepping stones in their careers, but they tend to measure the brilliance of their work by its length and its obtuseness. There are many great thinkers in the world of technology who have a far more detailed knowledge of what is being developed than James Martin, but they do not know how to communicate that fact in plain English – or do not want to. The books they write are for the tiny inner circles of their peer groups – not that that isn't a good reason to write a book, but it does make it harder to find a publisher because it limits the potential audience. In order to interest publishers, you need to be able to demonstrate that there will be a wide market for your words, and that can only be done if you are a good communicator, shedding light into previously darkened corners.

With a well-produced book from an established publisher you actually have something to sell to the media. You have a reason to be on chat shows and to be writing articles. You have behind you a tradition which has been built up over the last two centuries: people who write books should be listened to.

With the world-wide growth of literacy and technical developments in word-processing and printing, there are going to be more books appearing. They will have short life-spans and they will be more specialized and targeted. The days when you could write a text book and expect schools to be using it for 20, 30 or even 50 years are drawing to a close. Things are moving faster, which means that it will become harder to be heard above the competitive clamour. But it also means that there will be more and more opportunities for people with something to say to get published in one form or another.

There will always be 'big books' – the sort that catch the imagination of a wide audience at just the right time – as well as a plethora of smaller publishing opportunities which will provide the authors of these 'superbooks' with a useful training ground.

It is still hard to get published by a good publisher, but it is a goal which should be tackled in one way or another, and, with the right degrees of thought and perseverance, it is not impossible for anyone.

WHAT DO PUBLISHERS WANT?

Publishers always need writers with good ideas – a concept which is hard to grasp when you keep showering them with ideas which you think are good, only to have them rejected, seemingly out of hand, accompanied by little printed slips. Every now and then a kind editor will send a letter which shows they have actually read the manuscript you submitted to them, but their reasons for turning it down are nearly always a direct contradiction of whatever the last one said.

They do, however, need ideas and writers able to execute them, otherwise they will not have any products to sell. The terrible truth is that most of the ideas which most of us have most of the time are no good. They are either unoriginal, unworkable or unsaleable in one way or another. So the accent has to be on the word 'good'.

There are hundreds of publishers. Although many of them are owned by various large, international conglomerates, they still function as independent companies, making independent decisions about what they will or won't publish.

As a potential author, you must use all your marketing skills to persuade them, as the initial customer, that they should be buying your idea. You must convince them that you are capable of coming up with the goods, that there is a market for your writing and that no-one else has got there first. You're in just the same position as a company which manufactures chicken curries and which wants to sell its products through Marks and Spencer. The company believes the public wants what it has to sell, but until it can convince the buyers at M&S, it is impossible to reach the end consumer effectively.

It is hard to convince anyone of anything when you have no track record. Remember that you are basically asking a company to invest something around the equivalent of your entire year's earnings on a project for which you have no way of guaranteeing success. At least with the chicken curries M&S can take a few and then cancel the order if they don't sell; with books you are asking the customer (i.e. the publisher) to undertake all the costs of manufacture, most of which occur in the preparation of the text and the first print run, as well as the marketing – and still without a guaranteed sale of a single copy. No wonder they're cautious.

Before approaching a publisher, prepare a plan which will answer all the questions a publisher is likely to ask. If, for instance, you are a photographer and want to write a book on how to hire a professional photographer to undertake corporate assignments, you should be able to come up with some facts and figures on the market-place you are addressing. What is the rationale for the book? Could you, for instance, provide information which would show that interest in corporate photography exists in the market-place? Do you have some statistics for how much is spent annually by companies on photography? Is this figure increasing or decreasing? Who are your target market? Are they general management or just public relations, advertising and communications managers? Are there figures to show that large companies do more corporate photography than medium or small ones? What other titles are there in the market? Have they sold well or badly? How will your book differ from the others? What will be its unique selling point? What is your expertise in the subject? Have you written on the subject before? Do you have articles which you can show to the publisher to convince him or her that you are an expert? How long do you think the book should be? Should it be full of glossy pictures to illustrate the text or not? How long would it take you to complete the book? How much should it retail at?

Having answered these questions in your mind, you need to put together a proposal. Different publishers like to see different things, but you should basically do as much background work as possible. The more you have to show the publisher, the better your chances of making a sale. If you can afford the time, it might be worth writing the whole book before you approach anyone, but it would be better not to send the whole manuscript straight away.

Start with a series of chapter headings, explaining in each one what you are going to talk about and why it will be of use to the reader. Then write two or three sample chapters to prove that you can actually write (it is surprising how many people can't).

Most books need to be at least 50,000 words long, and many will go up to 80,000 or more. In some cases you might be able to make a case for fewer words, particularly if you can suggest useful illustrations and diagrams. But publishers still need to be convinced that you have the stamina to write an entire book.

Always bear in mind that there has to be a reason why a customer in a shop should pick up your book in the first place, pay money for it in the second place, and then actually read it from beginning to end. A publisher must be able to see how he or she is going to sell the copies which are printed.

If you can prove that your book will become a standard work of reference for every university or training course in your subject, or if you can produce a list of 5,000 names and addresses of people who have attended seminars which you have held and who have filled in forms saying that they would like to see a book on your subject, you are likely to find a red carpet stretched out from the publisher's office to the nearest expensive restaurant, because as far as they are concerned, that is the most important information.

APPROACHING A PUBLISHER

At the beginning of your career, the chances of any of your ideas being taken up by a publisher are slight, so it can't hurt for you to send the same idea to several at once. They can sometimes take months to reply to an idea, so if you laboriously send it to one at a time the idea will be out of date before you can find someone to publish it.

Start by browsing among the shelves of a bookshop which carries books in your sector. Make a note of every publisher who has produced something similar. There should be at least ten on your list, and if your subject is of general interest, it might be as many as 50.

Telephone each one and try to find the name of the editor who deals with your subject matter. Some publishers are very reluctant to give out names and will simply suggest that you write to the editorial department; others will be friendly and encouraging.

Send a copy of the synopsis and specimen chapter, with the return postage and a covering letter, then wait. If you haven't heard anything after two months, try ringing up and enquiring just in case they have lost it. On the whole, however, if they don't respond within that time, they are not interested and you would do better to spend your time finding other publishers to write to. Don't take offence at any rejections and rebuffs you receive. Getting published can take endless patience.

A publisher who likes your idea might ask you to do some more sample chapters, or to go in to see them. Go in a selling frame of mind. At no stage give them any reason to doubt that you are entirely confident that there is a market out there which is desperate to read your words. The editor you meet will have to put your idea to the salesforce and accountants – who make the final decisions on what does and doesn't get published. Giving them a strong enough case to work with will make them your champions at the publisher's meetings, which you will be excluded from.

Make it obvious that you have thought the whole project through and that you have a firm idea of where the market is. Let them know that you will be happy to undertake any publicity or promotional work necessary, and that you are so convinced of the book's eventual success that you are willing to work on a 'payment' system of royalties only. Most authors receive a small advance to help them survive during the time they are writing the book, and to demonstrate the publisher's commitment to the project. At this stage of your career, however, you are more interested in getting published than getting paid, and if you have a royalties agreement, you will receive your money in the long run anyway. If you offer to waive your advance, you have improved the editor's financial reasons for publishing the book, and strengthened the case which can be put to the sales and accounts departments.

Once you get the go-ahead from a publisher, don't bother to wait for their legal department to get the contract drawn up – start writing. The chances are you will have finished the book before they have finished drawing up your contract. It is possible that something will go wrong before the contract arrives and the whole project might collapse. If that is the case, you will still have had the experience of writing a whole book, and will now have a fuller manuscript to offer to another publisher.

In some cases, you will work right up to the end on a book with one publisher, only to have the project fall through for some reason (your editor might leave or the company might be bought by someone else), and once again you will have to hawk your manuscript around different publishers. It is a depressing business, but with each step you will be getting nearer to your goal, and learning a great deal along the way.

Some books are hard to sell as an abstract concept and you will need to write the whole manuscript before you start approaching publishers. If this is the case, always be prepared to make changes when the publisher wants them. There is no point in 'taking stands' at this stage. The important goal is to be published and to make working with you as pleasant and easy for the publisher as possible, so that they will want to do it again. If possible, learn to use a word-processor. It will make the chore of correcting and extending far less troublesome and make you more able to meet deadlines and to perform professionally.

There is no reason why you shouldn't be working on two different books with two different publishers at the same time – as long as the subject-matters do not clash. It would be best to own up when the books are about to come out, however, so that the publicity of both can be designed to feed off from each other.

Waiting for a reply
Once you have written the book and agreed any changes with your editor, there will then be a long wait before it is published – unless it is strictly topical, in which case the publishers will dazzle you with their speed. When there is a royal wedding it is amazing how many publishers are able to get books of the event into the shops within days, while a normal book might be grinding through their system for up to six months.

Be sure to meet the publicity departments that will be handling your book, and find out what they are planning to do. In most cases they will have a set pattern of working: sending out a certain number of review copies and publicizing the book in their catalogues. The chances are that unless you enthuse them with ideas your book will have been forgotten in a month, having been eclipsed by another set of new titles. Show them that you are willing to put yourself out. You might, for instance, be able to arrange a series of seminars in the month that the book comes out, which the press could be invited to, and at which the book could be heavily promoted.

Don't hesitate to take your own publicity initiatives, just as you have at the other stages in your climb to the top. Write to all the relevant editors telling them you are having the book published and asking if they would be interested in reading it/interviewing you/ having you write articles based on the subject matter. Enclose some blurb which explain why the book is important and relevant; and, as always, make sure they all have a new set of photographs of you, captioned with your name and telephone number and the fact that you are the author of the book (including the publisher's name and date of publication).

Show your hit-list of editors to your publisher's publicity people to see if they are planning to cover any or all of them. There will be no harm in both of you going to the same people as long as the approach is different. If they are sending out review copies and suggesting that you sould be interviewed, you could still be approaching the same editors with offers of articles. The closer you can work with the publisher the better, but the chances are that your personal publicity campaign will be more intensive and last longer than theirs. After all, you only have one product to sell, they have hundreds.

As soon as you have finished one book, start suggesting ideas for others. If you have proved yourself to be a good and reliable writer, they will be happy to listen. It might also be worth writing to other publishers after the book has come out, introducing yourself and telling them that you would be happy to discuss any ideas that they might have. It sometimes happens that a publisher will decide that they have a gap on their lists for books on corporate design or computer security, and will look around for somebody to write them. Make sure your name and number is in front of any editor likely to be in this position, and that they know you are already a published author.

If your publisher wants you to sign any sort of exclusivity deal, the time has come to start being more careful about contracts and financial details. If you are uncomfortable in negotiating with publishers, it might be worth hiring an agent beforehand, or at least finding a solicitor who specializes in looking after the affairs of authors. On the whole it is better to remain flexible and able to offer your products to the whole market-place, unless you find a publisher who provides the perfect partnership. Even then you need to bear in mind the fact that individuals move about and the editor you got on with so well on the first book may not be there for the second or third, or fourth.

PAYING TO BE PUBLISHED – VANITY OR SPONSORSHIP?

When large, respectable publishers do a deal with someone which involves them in contributing to the costs of publishing a book, it is known in the industry as 'sponsored publishing'. When a small, unknown publisher or printer does it, it is known as 'vanity publishing'. It is hard for someone on the outside to see the difference, and there is a place for both approaches under certain circumstances, but only after all other avenues have been explored.

Always *start* by trying to interest a publisher in your idea, and obtaining royalties and perhaps even an advance, just like a professional writer. If you are unable to do this, you can, as we have discussed, waive your advance.

You might also offer to buy a certain number of the books. Suppose, for instance, that you run sales training courses, and want to write a book which encapsulates your ideas and the methods you use. To have the book published by a reputable publisher will increase your credibility in the market-place, and the book would also be a nice thing to give, or possibly sell, to all the people who come on your courses. If, for instance, you are charging a delegate £200 for a day's training, it will not hurt to give him or her a paperback version of your book, which may only have cost you two or three pounds, and is a good public relations exercise.

If you have failed to convince a publisher to go ahead in the ideal way, but they have suggested that the idea is not impossible, a way should be found of minimizing their financial risk on the first print run. Think of ways in which you could use copies of the book yourself. Could you give it to customers? Could you sell it to employees? Could you send out massive mailings to the press or to the City to bolster your company's image or to prepare for flotation? If you can offer to buy a few thousand copies of the book from the publishers, you have completely changed the complexion of the deal. Although they won't earn anything from it unless they sell some copies themselves through the traditional outlets, they don't stand to *lose* anything if the book turns out to be a disaster. You, on the other hand, have gained the authority of their name on the spine of the book and the expertise of their editors and designers, as well as a few thousand copies of the book to sell or give away.

If all the reputable publishers still refuse to handle the project, it might be time to change your tack and think of other angles and approaches. If, however, you remain convinced that the book will be a useful marketing tool for yourself and your company, you can then start examining how much it would cost to pay for the whole project yourself, treating the book as a glorified corporate brochure or training manual.

You can then go back to the big-name publishers and ask them if they would be willing to undertake the editorial and printing work for you, and put their name to it, if you underwrite all the costs. If they think the book will do their reputations no harm, they may well agree to do this. If they think there is any danger that your book will undermine the credibility of their name in the marketplace, they will refuse, no matter how much you improve your offer.

Again, if you get a refusal, you must think seriously about whether you are on the right lines. There must be reasons why all these experienced people are telling you not to do it. If you are still convinced that you are right, the time has come to go to a vanity publisher – who could be any printer capable of handling the printing and binding of a book to your design.

Before you commit yourself to anything, however, be sure that the publisher can produce work of the standard you require, and be even more sure that you know what you are going to do with all the copies. There is nothing more humiliating than a warehouse full of books which have proved to be a money-wasting ego-trip.

You can give the book as Christmas presents to employees and customers. You can send them to the press and all the other contacts on your hit-list who may, or may not, guess that you have had to pay for publication. Provided you have done a good job on the text, and that the publisher has designed and printed it well, you have still created a marketable product, which will help you in your climb to the top.

Wess Roberts, an ex-Vice President of Human Resources at American Express, wrote a book called *The Leadership Secrets of Attila the Hun*, which he was unable to find a publisher for. He decided to publish some copies at his own expense, which he did, and went on to sell 8,000 of them from his home in America.

A friend suggested that he should send a copy to Ross Perot, the billionaire head of Dallas-based software company EDS, who was at the time very high profile, having formed his own commando unit to rescue two of his people who had been imprisoned in Iran after the revolution. Perot liked the book and ordered 700 copies.

When Perot's company was bought by General Motors, he was very unimpressed with the management of his new partners, and kept saying so in public. At one dinner attended by the GM management, Perot tried to distribute 500 copies of Roberts' book. GM Chairman Roger Smith prohibited it, and the incident was described in a book called *Call Me Roger* by Albert Lee. This brought the *Attila* book to the attention of Bantam Press who decided they would like to publish it as a major management title.

The moral of this tale is that if you truly believe in your book, and if it is a genuine reflection of all your beliefs and abilities, then perhaps you should let nothing dissuade you from publishing it.

On the whole, however, most of us do not have the time or the money to commit to such a major project, and it would be better to keep trying to be published in the traditional way for as long as possible, and then treat vanity publishing as little more than the production of a glorified corporate brochure. It might look like a book to the outside world, but to your accounts department it will simply be an advertising and promotional project.

HIRING A GHOST-WRITER

Not everyone has the time or inclination to write an entire book, or even an entire article. But that doesn't mean they shouldn't do it.

If you have the ideas, and you have the material which will provide the background, either in your head or in your files, then it is relatively easy to find someone who will undertake the mechanics of turning your material into an article or book.

Anyone who has undertaken any sort of training work, for instance, will have prepared notes of some sort. It may well be that those notes could be turned into a book. You might be able to do it yourself, but you might equally be so close to the subject that you can't see how to change the shape and structure to suit a different medium.

There are two ways of approaching a ghost-writing project. If you already have a working relationship with a publisher, you could show them the material and ask them if they think it could be done, and if so, do they know of a ghost-writer who could help you? If they say yes, then they will probably agree to pay the writer, and take the money out of whatever you would have earned had you written it all yourself. In most cases there won't be much money left for you, but then you have got a book under your name which you haven't had to expend much time or energy on producing. If you work out your daily rate for doing whatever your normal job is, and then assume that you would have had to take three solid months off work to write a book, you can soon see how economical it might be to pay someone else to do it for you.

In most cases, sitting down and talking to the ghost-writer for two weekends will give them enough material to produce a book with no written background material at all.

Alternatively, you might hire the ghost-writer yourself, to help you get the material into a good enough state to show to publishers. A writer might, for instance, go through all your course notes with you and suggest how they can be structured into chapter headings, and can go away and write the sample chapters needed to convince a publisher to go ahead. You might choose at that stage to tell the publisher that you are collaborating with someone else, or you could just hand over the manuscript, having already read it through and checked that there is nothing in it which you wouldn't be willing to have going out under your name, and allow the publisher, like the reader, to assume it is all your own work.

In some cases the ghost-writer will get his or her name alongside yours. In some cases the ghost-writer may demand the billing, in others it is the 'author' who doesn't want to be accused later of trying to pass off another's work as his or her own. More often, however, the ghost-writer remains invisible.

YOUR BIOGRAPHY

Another use for books is to have them written about you. If you have reached a stage in your career where it is possible that you could interest a publisher with a story about your life, you could try writing an autobiography, or you could hire a writer to do a biography of you. If you hire a writer, it would be wise to choose someone you have already worked with for a project as personal and sensitive as this. But if you don't know anyone, then you will have to rely on your publisher's judgment.

If you have reached this height, however, you may have started to draw back from publicity rather than court it. There are many famous people who are continually being approached by publishers who would like them to write their stories, and continually being offered the services of ghost-writers to make the process easier for them. In some cases, they feel they still have too much to achieve and that a book would be premature; in others, they simply don't want to expose that much of themselves to the public gaze.

At certain stages of your career, however, it could be a good move to set up a biography of yourself, making it financially viable for a reputable publisher to take it on by guaranteeing to take a number of copies, as discussed earlier.

EXPLOITING PUBLICATION

We have already talked a little about how to make sure that your book receives maximum publicity when it comes out. It is important to ensure that you maintain the momentum for as long as the material is relevant. Always have a stock of copies which you can give to anyone who shows an interest in your work, from potential customers to journalists who are interviewing you. If your publisher announces that it is planning to remainder your book (that means it is giving up hope of selling all the copies at the normal price, and is going to be selling the rest off at a massive discount to discount book shops or whoever else will buy it), then try to buy as many copies of it as you can afford. If it is a decent book, you will always be able to find uses for it.

Organize conferences and seminars around your book's contents, and never be afraid to re-cycle some of the thoughts within the book as articles, updating and changing them to suit the situation. Whenever you are asked to give brief details of who you are, include details of the book – 'John Smith, Managing Director of Smith Industries and author of *How to Run a Green Company*, published by International Publishing Corp'.

When the book first comes out, offer to talk to the publisher's sales-force, to enthuse them for the product and to answer any questions they might have. They are going to be the ones trying to convince booksellers to stock large numbers of your book, and to put up point-of-sale material, so the more they know about the book and the more they believe in its value, the better the selling job they will do.

Be aware also of the potential for exploitation in the opposite direction. For instance, if you have the chance to do a television programme, then explore the possibilities of producing a book of the programme. Michael Palin's book of his *Around the World in 80 Days* series for the BBC was the best selling book of 1989, and there are numerous examples of other publishing exercises which cash in on someone's fame: cookery books, gardening books, sport and show-business biographies, accounts of financial scandals or great news stories.

When Richard Branson set off to Japan with the intention of flying a balloon across the Pacific, a writer was lined up to produce a 'book of the trip'. The fact that the trip was aborted for technical reasons meant that there wasn't a story to write – on that occasion – but whenever Branson sets out on an adventure there is likely to be a story worth telling, and a book becomes a lynchpin in an orchestrated marketing exercise – marketing the event, marketing Branson, marketing Branson's companies.

CHAPTER EIGHT

Using Your Lifestyle

IF YOU HAVE got this far on the road to fame, the time has probably come to ask yourself whether you want to go any further. You are now established as an expert in your field. You have a reputation which means that you can get almost any job you want within your sector, and also earn a considerable amount of extra money from your activities 'on the side'.

You have written books which are earning royalties, you earn appearance fees for seminars and editors pay you for your articles. When you appear on television or radio you are handsomely rewarded. Your professional life is probably going pretty well and, like most ambitious people, you may have a hard time balancing the demands of your work with the demands of your home life.

Stop and think carefully whether you really want to endanger all this. Do you sincerely want to be famous? Do you want to be a familiar face to everyone you pass in the street or supermarket? Do you want to be unable to use public transport without someone buttonholing you with their problems and wanting your autograph?

Once you have become famous you will always stand out from the crowd. You won't be able to have a quiet game of golf with a friend or attend a family wedding or funeral, without people noticing that you are there and making a fuss of you at the expense of your friends and relatives. You will not be able to eat in your favourite restaurant without feeling eyes upon you; if you have a row with your spouse in public, you run the risk of reading all about it in the next morning's papers.

The trouble with being a big-time celebrity is that the media and the public are as likely to put you down as they are to praise you. Most politicians and actors are used to this sort of treatment, as are the members of the Royal Family who attract the most attention. Senior businesspeople are also having to get used to the rollercoaster of fashion. John Egan was one of the most celebrated businesspeople in the country when he first brought Jaguar out from under British Leyland. A few years later the company's shareholders were turning on him for selling out to Ford. Freddie Laker and John de Lorean suffered even greater swings in popularity.

If you are willing to move on to the status of full-blown celebrity, you have to use your personal life as part of the image-building exercise.

RUMOUR OR REALITY

It may be that merely allowing rumours to circulate about your private life will endow it with more glamour than if it is spread out before people in full colour. Not everyone, however, wants to wait until opportunities for publicity fall into their laps. Many successful people want to flaunt their achievements. They want to show off their houses and spouses, their swimming pools and Rolls Royces; they want to talk to journalists about their prowess on the rugby fields or their ability to cross the Atlantic single-handed. Mickie Most, the pop music promoter, has had more publicity for his new palazzo in North London in recent years than most of his pop stars; both Peter de Savary and Alan Bond put their names on the front pages of the world's newspapers with their attempts at the America's Cup.

The greatest exponent of this type of publicity, however, has to be Richard Branson, who somehow manages to have the media with him wherever he goes, and to continually think up new things for them to write about. He has all the trappings of the tycoon, from the stately home in England to the private Caribbean Island, but he has succeeded in making himself *seem* like an adventurer and a 'boy next door' figure through his escapades in boats and balloons. His policy of complete openness with the media and the public seems, so far, to have paid off. He is a genius at *making himself interesting*.

WHAT MAKES CELEBRITIES INTERESTING?

When someone goes to interview Branson they might find him on his house boat in London, or on one of his aircraft flying to America, or preparing for a balloon flight. In all these situations, the interviewer is bound to end up writing more than if he or she was received by other record company tycoons merely in their offices for an hour.

In fact, you hear comparatively little about what is actually happening at Virgin, except when Branson decided to go public, and then decided to buy the company back because the stock market is consistently under-rating it. It is assumed that it is a well-run company which would still be well-run even if Branson himself was killed on one of his mad-cap adventures. He makes the company interesting by being interesting himself, by fulfilling the dreams of others, by being larger than life and, to most people, likeable.

But you don't have to be in a glamorous industry to achieve such fame. Ted Toleman is Chairman of the Toleman Group, a family company which based its fortunes on vehicle distribution, and which also owns companies which make other products ranging from boats to socks. Toleman bought a controlling interest in Cougar, the company which built the Atlantic Challenger which

Toleman and Branson took across the Atlantic in an attempt to break a record. When the boat was holed by some submerged debris 93 miles from the finishing line, *both* men were front page news as they were fished out of the ocean. Toleman has gone on to pursue other adventures and feats of endurance, while also gaining a reputation for a lavish lifestyle at home.

This sort of high profile behaviour can, of course, backfire. It is hard to convince your union leaders that they should settle for a five per cent pay-rise if you are in the papers for spending hundreds of thousands of pounds on a new house or an international party. The trick is to find a lifestyle which is interesting and glamorous, but in keeping with your professional interests.

Stars of the fashionable world have an easier time of it since they are *expected* to be outrageous and glamorous. Designers, photographers, writers and artists are all expected to be larger than life. Norman Parkinson could live on a mountain top in Tobago, Mick Jagger and Jerry Hall can do whatever they like, because that is what is expected of them. David Hicks and Tricia Guild, both designers, allow books and articles featuring their own houses and gardens to appear: their lifestyles are their shop windows. Cecil Beaton had a home which reflected exactly the elegance and luxury of his whole lifestyle.

Sometimes, a celebrity's lifestyle can include the whole family. The Kennedys, in their rise to power in America, did all they could to spread stories of how they brought up their children to be world leaders. The public loved it – it was soap opera on the grandest scale. Was there ever such a big story as the assassination of John F Kennedy and the marriage of his beautiful young widow to Onassis, one of the richest men in the world? In due course the image changed: various members of the family proved themselves to have feet of clay, and revelations about JFK's sex life and personal morality changed the picture. But interest in their family lifestyle remains.

The Forte family, the Hefners, the Guinnesses – all convey a certain style which, although it sometimes backfires on them, continues to keep them in the news. It is the sort of publicity which – good or bad – *demonstrates that you have arrived.*

Many people already have personal stories which provide the necessary background, yet simply don't realize it because the stories have evolved gradually and don't seem unusual to the participants. Stories that involve personal striving and achievement against the odds (which will cover just about everyone who has got this far in the race for fame) are what people want to hear. They want to hear about best-selling novelists who had their greatest works rejected by 20 publishers before they finally made it into print. They want to hear about multi-millionaires who lost several fortunes before finally making it back. They want to hear stories of personal tragedy and courage, battles against cancer, the loss of a child, broken hearts and miracle cures.

All the material that makes good novels and films, plays and songs, makes good background material for people who want to be famous. It provides the media with the material it needs to keep its audiences entertained.

MAKING YOURSELF INTERESTING

Once you have decided that you really do want to be a celebrity, and have decided which parts of your life you are willing to share with the public, and which bits you are willing to hide and risk having un-covered at an embarrassing moment, you can then start to build your background story.

Start by trying to give an extra angle and level of interest to every interview or article that you are involved with. If you are going to be interviewed by a trade journalist, don't just meet him or her in your office, arrange to meet on the floor of your factory, or when you are making a tour of inspection of some part of your business.

If you are giving a general interview on yourself, do the same: take the journalist out for a round of golf if that is your hobby (he or she does not have to to play, but just watch), or show him or her round your house and garden if that is your pride and joy. Introduce the journalist to your family or to colleagues who will help to flesh out your story. The fact that you are a millionaire and your father was an out of work miner is going to give another human angle to the story, as will the fact that you and your spouse had to elope because your father-in-law-to-be didn't believe you had a future. Try to look at your life like a novel, and see which parts would be of most interest if you were the reader.

At the same time you must ruthlessly exorcize the boring bits: the worst thing you can do is bore your audiences. They don't want to know about the years of tedium and hard work that went into your success, they want the key points.

The more you give a journalist to write about, the more colourful and interesting the article will be. A profile of you that was destined to be a second feature might be elevated to a cover story if you give the press meaty enough material and photo opportunities. It may be that you don't want to give the impression to the working world that you spend too much time at leisure, so make sure that you keep a balanced picture and that you aren't always being pictured lying around swimming pools or drinking at the golf club.

Give the press opportunities to see you in action. Take a journalist with you to a client presentation or a board meeting, if no-one objects. Let him or her see you losing your temper and arguing about something you feel strongly about, or laughing at something which entertains you.

Don't do any of these things if they don't come naturally, because the press will be very quick to pick up any signs of falseness. It's simply a case of making the press see the side of you which you want the public to see.

When President Nixon's advisers decided that he should have a more relaxed image, they invited a number of press photographers to hide on the cliffs above his holiday home, and get 'candid' shots of the President walking his dog on the beach. Unfortunately no-one warned the President that he would look ridiculous if he did it in his normal business suit and shoes. It was obviously a set-up and simply made the photographers laugh.

Sit down and write a brief life history of yourself and your family. It only has to be a sketch of the key points and it is only for your own memory. Search your past for things which you think would be of interest to other people. As a teenager you may have bicycled across a desert or climbed a mountain in Japan. You may be an expert in chamber music or a brilliant amateur photographer. Whatever your passion, whether it is antique cars or modern art, flying helicopters or running marathons, breeding cats or ballroom dancing, people will be interested to know about it, and it will help to build a full picture of you in their minds as a character on the media stage.

By talking about other aspects of your life, you will give yourself another dimension in the eyes of both journalists and their readers. Why else does Richard Branson get so many more column inches than any other business leader? Why do the media keep on talking to Peter de Savary when there are hundreds of businesspeople with more successful careers? The answer is that they are interesting, rounded figures, whom everyone can relate to in different ways. They have both fulfilled common dreams by having adventures and growing rich.

Flaunting it

Whether or not you want to flaunt your worldly success depends on what business you are in, and who your public is. If you are a successful doctor, it might not be tasteful to show off too much wealth, whereas a pop promoter can be as flash as he or she likes.

If you would like to show your home to the public, either because you are in the design or building business and it is a good example of your work, or because it reflects your lifestyle and philosophy in some way, the best place to start is with the women's and home interest magazines. The national media and colour supplements also need good stories on houses, gardens, boats and exotic cars. People like Terence Conran, Tricia Guild and Anita Roddick, whose businesses epitomize a certain style and way of life, can benefit enormously from allowing the cameras to glimpse inside their gates and front doors and from showing that they live as they preach.

If you are building a home from scratch, planning to convert a ruin or doing anything dramatic, try to involve a magazine – or even a television company – in the project from the start. Send them copies of the plans and photographs of what is currently there. Invite them down to see the 'before' and paint a tempting picture of how the 'after' will be. The actual transformation will provide the editors or producers with a much stronger story than if you only invite them once the whole thing is finished.

If you think your existing home or garden would be of interest to magazines, send them pictures and some brief details and invite editors to come and see it.

You are never going to be able to guard completely against the risk of a scandal hitting you (more about this in Chapter 11), but the more open and welcoming you are to the media in the good times, the less likely they are to start rooting about in the dustbin looking for evidence of clandestine vices.

We started the book by looking upon the process of becoming famous as a marketing exercise, with you as the product. If you have got this far, you are now equivalent to an established brand on the shelves. You must continue to find ways to improve the product and to imbue it with new unique selling points, otherwise it will soon begin to look old-fashioned and dull. If, for instance, you become involved with a charity, then do it in a big way, raising funds in public and having your name associated with it. If you get married (and your spouse is agreeable), do it in the full glare of the spotlight. When things are not going so well it is harder to talk to the media and see your story spread around, but it still helps to give a rounded picture and to keep the public on your side. Judy Garland's drinking problem was public because it couldn't be hidden, but her popularity continued, and if anything, her personal problems have added to the legend.

If fame is forcing itself upon you, as it does with royalty and some sports and showbusiness people, then there will doubtless be areas of your life which you want to keep completely hidden from the public gaze. For most readers of this book, however, fame is going to be something which you will have to strive for, and the more ammunition you can find, the more likely you are to be successful. Those who dedicate their lives to being famous, like Jeffrey Archer, Barbara Cartland and Richard Branson, generally succeed.

CHAPTER NINE

Creating the Right Image

MANY PEOPLE HAVE a built-in resistance to the idea of deliberately creating an image for themselves, but we all do it. We all want to create some sort of impression, even if it is the impression that we don't care about our image.

There are two reasons why you might want to think about your image. The first is that many people judge on first impressions. If you look important, they will assume that you are, until you prove them wrong. If you look insignificant, you will then have to labour to overcome prejudices and barriers in order to prove that you are someone who should be listened to.

The second reason is that you need to stand out from the crowd, if only in some minor way. You need to leave your various audiences with an impression of you which they will remember, a trade mark and a distinctive look which will make you instantly recognizable.

Some people are willing to go to greater lengths than others. John de Lorean, on his way to becoming one of the most famous, and infamous, figures in the motor industry, is reputed to have taken some pretty drastic measures. He underwent plastic surgery and chin implants to square up his jaw, and used hair technology to rid himself of a widow's peak which he didn't think looked powerful enough. He also lost weight and, for some extraordinary reason, shaved his legs. The result, however, was quite impressive: most people can remember the dashing, film star figure with the shock of white hair who looked for a time as if he was going to be one of the pioneers of the luxury car market, and then turned out to be living a life even closer to a film script, allegedly in league with drug barons and seen in court with his glamorous model wife.

Mrs Thatcher has also had a great deal of media attention focused on the cosmetic changes she has undergone since she first came to power. Her hair has softened, her teeth have been straightened, her voice has been re-trained and she has adopted a style of dress which conveys appropriate power signals without being unfeminine.

Now that the House of Commons is being televised, a number of grooming advisers are offering their services to members of parliament who want to look right in front of their audiences, advising them on how to dress, what to do with their hair and how to speak.

Some self-improvement gurus would suggest that anyone who is ambitious should pay attention to their appearance. If you want to be successful, they say, you should look successful. Aristotle Onassis was often quoted as saying that the first thing to acquire if you wanted to look rich was a suntan.

In some cases it might be *lack* of clothes which makes someone memorable – certainly in the pin-up modelling world, and at the more superficial end of the acting profession. Unusual people sometimes decide to use nudity as an attention getter. When *Cosmopolitan* decided in the 1970s to run male nudes for its readers, the first person to volunteer to appear was Vidal Sassoon. At that time the hairdressing industry, and Sassoon in particular, was moving into the business of general grooming, an industry which was about to take off in a big way, and this gave him a controversial opportunity to show off his own body and to make himself remembered.

Not everyone can become arbiters of style, even if they want to. Bjorn Borg, the tennis star, invested in a number of businesses when he retired from the court, one of which was clothing and leisurewear. However good a tennis player he was, few could say that Borg cut a particularly dashing figure when dressed for the street – this part of his business did not thrive. While he was playing, however, and always pictured in the press and on the television, he was able to use his long hair and sweat bands to create a trademark which could be instantly recognized and remembered.

Using clothes as badges of office is as old as civilization. We can tell when we are looking at religious leaders, kings and judges by their costumes. When we are confronted by an army of people who are hard to define, like the battalions of Japanese businessmen beavering away in western countries and western clothing, we are unnerved and unsure of who we are dealing with.

TAKE A LOOK AT YOURSELF

Start to cultivate your image by looking dispassionately at yourself. Don't just look in the mirror: you are used to seeing your own reflection and you will make allowances through familiarity. We all get used to looking at our friends and relatives, and find it hard to imagine what impression they would make if we met them for the first time now. We are even more familiar with our own reflections.

Look at pictures of yourself and, if possible, moving images, like films and videos. Believe the bad ones as well as the good. It is all too easy to dismiss a photograph of oneself as being 'ghastly' just because it doesn't live up to your own self-image. Other people don't just see the posed, full face with a half smile that you put towards a camera when you know that you are posing. They see you full face, side on and backview. They see you laughing with your mouth wide open, teeth and gums on full show. They see you with your eyes screwed up and the wind lifting your hair to show carefully concealed bald patches. You must be aware of all these things so that you can do something about the 'faults' which are correctable and learn to use some of your personal assets.

If you are not honest with yourself about your weak points as well as your strong ones, you will not be able to improve on them or put them right. You have got to find a style which puts across the right messages about you, which you feel confident with, and which suits you.

WHAT TO WEAR

There are two stages in choosing what you are going to wear when you are in front of your audiences. The first involves conforming to the basic uniform that they expect to see you in; the second involves making some dramatic difference to your appearance that marks you out as an individual and makes you memorable. When people first see you, they need to feel comfortable that you are what they expected: a successful lawyer, a modernistic architect or a lecturer on anthropology.

There are some people, particularly in showbusiness, who use clothes to bring their talents to the attention of the public, and in some cases to disguise their paucity of talent.

Liberace is a prime example of someone whose clothes became more important than his expertise at the piano. There were thousands of people who could play as well as him, but there was only one Liberace.

Elton John started in the same way, with his outrageous costumes and spectacles, but in his case the costumes have gradually been toned down as his position as a performer has become more certain.

After a while you don't have to worry about your appearance – you have arrived, and people will take notice of you, whatever you wear. Not many people reach that happy stage, and usually they have grown so used to the clothes they have worn on the way up, that it doesn't occur to them to change them once they have reached their goal.

The clothes you wear may be partly dictated by your shape. (Demis Roussos supposedly wore Kaftans to hide his enormous bulk.) There are certain styles which merely accentuate someone's girth, lack of height, stoop or other physical characteristics which they might prefer instead to disguise.

So start by deciding what you can and can't wear, and then turn your mind to what it is that your audience will be impressed by.

Sometimes there will be very definite reasons for buying clothes where you do. (Ralph Halpern, chairman of the Burton Group, used to buy his suits at Burton, until the company bought the up-market department store Harvey Nichols, and he was able to dress in a style more suited to one of the highest-paid managers in the country, while still being loyal to his own brands.) The trick is to make sure that once you have chosen your style you create it thoroughly. If you are going to look like a serious businessperson, then wear well-tailored pin-stripes and not just ordinary grey business suits. If you are going to be a showman, then go for suits of evangelical white, or flourescent pink if it's suitable, not just a pink shirt and tie.

Once you have found a style which suits your personality and image, stick with it. Don't waste time trying out different things. If you are ambitious and hard-working, you won't have the time to spend window shopping, so do your thinking and your research at the beginning, and buy (or have made) the best clothes available in your style. That way you will never be made to feel inferior by the people who come to learn from you, and you will also get better value for money in the long run because your clothes will last longer. You will also save time when you go out shopping for replacements.

Colour can sometimes become a trademark. Diana Moran, an exercise teacher who appeared on breakfast television, became known in the popular press as 'The Green Goddess' because of her green tracksuits. She was wearing the uniform which was expected of her profession, but by choosing an unusual colour and by being consistent, she turned it into a trademark.

You can carry your style of dress into the realms of eccentricity if you feel it is suitable. If you run a formal restaurant, you could dress in frock coat and knee-britches, provided you don't feel a fool. It is easy to mock such fancy dress, but it is memorable and marks out the establishments which use it, such as Coutts Bank, as having certain traditional values.

If you are in the oil business and want to effect the airs of a Texan, there is no reason why you shouldn't wear a ten-gallon hat and cow-boy boots. If you want to go a stage further, you could arrive at work in a pick-up truck – a small touch which would soon become well-known and talked about because of its apparent incongruity.

Decide what you are. Are you a mad professor or an English country gentleman? Are you a daughter of the aristocracy or a gypsy girl who has fought for respectability? Whatever the story, dress accordingly, and make sure that it is carried right through your wardrobe. It is no good buying expensive Savile Row suits and pulling on a plastic mac the moment it rains; you have to be consistent – from your hand-made shoes to your cashmere scarf.

The clothes, of course, are only part of the image, and you need to be sure that you can carry it through and not be exposed as a fraud and poseur. Don't pretend to be a country gentleman if you haven't got the house, Range Rover and labradors to match when the photographers come to call. It is no good dressing like a Mayfair dandy out for a night at the Ritz, if you live in a semi-detached house in Surbiton. Be yourself and be truthful, but try to do it with style.

Finding a gimmick

Once you have perfected the basic uniform, you can look for the finishing touch which will just lift you out of the ordinary. It might mean wearing a bow tie when everyone else wears ordinary ones, like Robin Day. It might be an elaborately embroidered waistcoat or hat. Whatever it is, it must be distinctive and consistent. It must suit you and you must try not to be photographed without it.

When trying to think what to use, start at the top and work down. What about your hair? John Harvey Jones, ex-chairman of ICI, made his long hair a trademark simply because all the other senior businessmen of his stature and generation were balding or had short-back-and-sides. He also added the touch of some unspeakably gaudy ties, which most ambitious people would avoid, imagining that they would merely suggest that the wearer didn't know what good taste was all about. Harvey Jones didn't have to worry about that. He was confident that he could do the job, and went on to prove it. The hair and ties became instantly recognizable throughout the business world, and later on national television, just like Richard Branson's beard and sixties haircut.

A *lack* of hair can also be a trademark, as with Duncan Goodhew and Yul Brynner, and it is usually better to flaunt it than to try to hide it, as Arthur Scargill and Paul Daniels did – merely proving that they were not only ageing and balding, but perhaps vain and insecure as well.

There are infinite varieties of hairstyle which might help you stand out from the crowd: from pony tails for men to shaven heads for women; from outrageous dyes as used by Jimmy Saville when he was at the beginning of his career and working to be noticed, to eccentric, individual styles like Liza Minelli's.

Some people use smoking as a gimmick, like Noel Coward with the cigarette holder, although this is becoming less acceptable. Lew Grade became famous for the size of his cigars, which had the added effect of demonstrating that he was a movie mogul and extremely rich. His nephew, Michael Grade, has gone for the 1980s equivalent of power status symbols, the bold red braces, which are frequently photographed because he is seen working in his office with his jacket off, giving more signals of dynamism.

Spectacles can be a useful prop, as demonstrated by the snooker player Dennis Taylor, Dame Edna Everidge and Elton John. If you are going for the 'elder statesman/chairman of the board' look, it might be worth getting some half-moon glasses which instantly add an air of wisdom and years. There are a number of eccentric variations, like monocles and dark glasses (a favourite of pop singers and films stars).

If you are going to be famous, it helps if you can give the cartoonists something to work with, whether it is for your company newspaper, trade magazine or the *Daily Mail*. To be instantly recognized for your beard, your make-up or your style of dress helps to lift you from the crowd, and continues the process of imprinting you on the minds of varied audiences.

If you ride a lot, then use horses and riding clothes as your trademark; if you fly a private jet, then be photographed doing it, and dress to fit the part. Your style of dress can also have commercial advantages. Paloma Picasso, with her dramatic hair and make-up, is a living symbol of her brand of perfume.

SELLING YOUR IMAGE ON

Just as marketing people in the fast-moving-consumer-goods areas find that they have created a really strong brand (like Andrex toilet tissue or Mars Bars) and then use the branding to endorse other products (facial tissues for Andrex, ice cream bars for Mars), a successful celebrity can build an image which is suitable for endorsing other products.

Outrageous examples of this include Michael Jackson being paid a reported $15 million dollars to link his name with Pepsi (even though he didn't actually have to drink the product), but the same principles can work for a DIY expert recommending a new power tool.

Anyone who becomes famous for being an authority on a certain subject, or simply for having a certain image, can be used as an advertising vehicle. We have seen Orson Welles selling sherry and David Niven selling instant coffee, Stirling Moss selling cars and Jackie Stewart selling credit cards, Katie Boyle talking about Palmolive soap and Nanette Newman about Fairy Liquid.

Frederick Forsyth can endorse Rolex watches because he is known to have become a millionaire from his books, because his work reflects a manly, action-packed life, and because he himself once worked in the rough, tough, fast world of front page news reporting. All the right signals are there and the product benefits from being associated with him. A scholarly writer of historical fiction would not have the same appeal.

Because Bob Geldof is famous for his dishevelled and unshaven appearance, he was able to advertise disposable razor blades. Because he is associated with a great work of charity, bringing nutrition and life to those who were starving, he could also advertise milk. An anonymous charity worker in a safari jacket and horn-rimmed spectacles, who had worked for years in the back office at Oxfam, could have done neither.

At another level, gardening experts who are trusted by their public can endorse bulb catalogues and gardening books, and retired newsreaders can put their name to hearing aids and cat food.

Anyone who has worked hard at establishing a reputation for themselves in any field, will at some stage be able to find ways of selling that reputation on to commercial interests, but only if they have been able to make themselves known, recognizable and memorable to the public. Mark McCormack's multi-million pound business has made it possible for the sportspeople under his care to earn more after their sporting careers are over than they ever did at their peak. He has since expanded his skills to cover all types of public personalities.

Whether you *want* to do this kind of work is another matter, since you always run the risk of no longer being trusted as an impartial adviser, but seen instead as someone with vested interests to protect. You must decide for yourself when it is the right time to start cashing in on your life's work.

CHAPTER TEN

Being Talked About

THE PEOPLE THAT the gossip columnists most want to talk about are often the people who least want to see any details about their lives in print. Consequently, those who want to get into the columns have a hard time because the very fact that they want to be there makes them ineligible for it – almost.

Being talked about in the gossip columns lets people know that you have reached a certain status in life. The casual reader assumes that you must be either rich or famous to be written about.

The problem is that you can't choose what the press will write about you. You might want to talk about the fact that you have just signed a publishing contract for a million dollars; they may prefer to talk about the fact that the lady you are with is not your wife.

If you are in a sensitive sector, like politics, the church or banking, it would be safer not to court gossip columnists unless you are confident that you can handle the consequences. If, however, you believe, as many do, that the only thing worse than having bad things said about you is having no-one saying anything, then you can start chasing the publicity in the knowledge that anything is better than nothing.

Some people automatically get talked about because of who they are, i.e. the Royal Family, people in prominent jobs and anyone who is rich and famous, or related to someone rich and famous. Apart from the Royal Family, most of these people can avoid gossip most of the time regarding their personal lives. All they have to do is make sure that they don't go to the sort of events which the columnists and their suppliers of information go to, and that they lead exemplary private lives. (They cannot, however, always control those around them, and we will talk more about that in the next chapter.)

There are some people who can easily get themselves talked about because they have interesting personalities. They are probably rich and/or famous as well, because at least two of these three ingredients frequently go together, but it is their personalities rather than their achievements which make them interesting gossip fodder. Gossip columnists are not interested in how hard you worked to build your personal fortune, and will dismiss the whole process in a few words – 'The woman who made her fortune in coloured bidets', or 'The man who built a fortune on the proceeds of three divorce settlements'.

What the columnists are interested in is what you do at a more trivial level. Do you go fishing with the Prince of Wales? Do you get kissed by the Princess of Wales? Do you throw bread rolls and de-bag waiters in South Kensington restaurants? Do you 'sleep with people you shouldn't', and dance the night away in Jermyn Street or Berkeley Square? Do you have your house decorated by a relative of the Shah of Iran, and does your daughter really spend a thousand pounds a week on cocaine?

If you are sufficiently interesting, you will be written about, but only if you make yourself visible. Gossip columnists are not in-depth reporters spending weeks digging out the true facts about a story: they are listening to tittle tattle and passing it on. If you don't get drawn to their attention, the chances are you will pass unnoticed.

BECOMING A PARTY-GOER

The gossip columns are filled in two ways: firstly, with the items which the journalists themselves witness or hear about; secondly, with pieces given to them by people who attend the parties that they can't be at. You yourself may have to become one of the latter breed, at least to start with.

If you are consistently witty at celebrity dinner parties, you will find that your words and anecdotes will eventually reach the media. Likewise, if you are consistently drunk and abusive at parties given by the rich and famous, that will also get back.

There is no longer one set of high society people. Gossip-mongers deal in stories about pin-up models, hairdressers and estate agents as well as dukes and princesses, so there is no single round of parties which you have to get to in order to be noticed. In fact, it could actually hamper you to get too high in the social strata, since you may feel duty-bound to be more discreet about what is happening around you.

Being a friend of the Royal Family seldom does any harm to anyone if the friendship is uncovered by the press, but if those people were to talk indiscreetly about things that had been said to them, or about the private lives of their friends, they would soon find them-selves out in the cold.

It is better to stay in a social circle where you are comfortable and influential, and try to make that circle as interesting as you can to the media. This generally means spending a lot of money, although it can be done with only modest outlay if you are imaginative. The late Malcolm Forbes, publisher of *Forbes* magazine and friend of Eliza-beth Taylor, managed to raise his birthday party in 1989 out of the gossip columns on to the feature pages of the world's media by simply spending more money than anyone had ever spent on a party. He filled jumbos and private jets with the biggest names of the inter-national jet set (many of them advertising clients of his magazine empire), and flew them to his home in Morocco, where the most lavish banquet was thrown in a series of tents, with Elizabeth Taylor acting as hostess for the occasion.

Forbes had, however, put in a lot of groundwork before he was able to reach such giddy heights. He started by running a good company: the *Forbes* magazine is one of the most successful business magazines in America. He then went on to make himself extremely interesting. He rode motor bikes and flew in hot air balloons. He owned castles and chateaux all over the world and went to Scotland on a highly publicized mission to find his ancestors' bones. He had cultivated the right contacts at the highest levels and had become known to the columnists for his antics over many years.

Few people are able to dedicate quite so much money and time to building a famous lifestyle for themselves. Publishers of newspapers and magazines are particularly able at doing it, and usually have particularly large egos in the first place. Hugh Hefner and Bob Guccione have both spent much of their lives building lifestyles which reflect the philosophies of their magazines, *Playboy* and *Penthouse*. Robert Maxwell has also put a great deal of effort into promoting himself as a media giant.

If you feel that being talked about in gossip columns will help your business, then you will have to be prepared to be thick-skinned about how you approach it. You are basically going to have to keep showering the media with information about yourself until they become so used to your name that they begin to think of you as someone well-known, or at least as someone interesting.

PLAYING HOST

If you are throwing a party which some celebrities will attend, try to make it imaginative: make it fancy dress, or hold it on the roof of your office with a full dance band. Whatever you do, make sure you send invitations to the relevant diarists, and hire a photographer to cover the event – someone who is equipped to turn photographs round in a few hours, so that they can be delivered to the daily media in time for the next morning's editions.

Of course, it's better if the papers send their own photographers, but that can't be guaranteed, so you must make sure that someone is recording the event pictorially. Once the party is under way, someone should ring the papers who haven't shown up to tell them who is there, and any interesting snippets. When Anna Ford, who had just been sacked by breakfast television, threw a glass of wine over the man who had sacked her at a party, the story was heard by everyone in the media. It helped to publicize what was happening at the station, and it also reinforced Anna Ford's image as a strong woman with a mind of her own. Any fights or arguments, or anyone well-known who is there with a new partner, is going to be of interest to the columnists.

Before the event, send a press release to all relevant media, saying who is invited, how much it has cost (if that is relevant) and why the party is being held, so that the media have the information to hand.

It's also worth hiring a production company to make a video, copies of which could be given to guests later as souvenirs. A video means that the night is captured in the archives for later use. A few shots might also be a useful part of a corporate video, or might be useful to a television company making a programme about you or your company at a later date. The more material you have on record of yourself as you rise to the top, the better the coverage of you once you have got there. (The danger of this attitude, of course, is that when you get to the top you may be embarrassed by the things you had to do to get there, and might prefer it if there weren't any video records of you in anything less than an all-commanding position.)

After the event is over, it might be worth sending sets of pictures and written details of what happened to the magazines which are likely to be interested – by the next day it will be too late to go to the nationals.

If you are eating in a restaurant which is well-known to the gossip columnists and something unusual happens, the chances are that they will get to hear about it, and will report it in their pages. Don't hesitate to ring them and tell them about it anyway, just in case they miss it. They need people who are in the right places all the time to feed them with stories. If you prove to be a reliable source, they will be keener to co-operate with giving you the publicity you think you need.

Gossip isn't limited to the national press. Most trade papers have some sort of diary or events pages, and they need interesting pictorial material more than the nationals. If possible, invite the editors of the magazines which are of interest to you to the party and supply them with pictures to take away. If that doesn't work, send them a complete account the next day, with pictures. Make sure there is a picture of you, and that you are clearly captioned as the host.

A story which starts in a gossip column may well grow into a full-blown news story. If you were to swap wives or husbands with someone famous, it might make an item in a gossip column in one of the up-market papers. All gossip columnists read one another's pages to see if they have missed anything, and one of the more down-market publications might decide that the story needed more investigation, after which they could blow it up for the front page. Newspapers keep extensive files of material they have published, so when the time comes for a journalist to write a full-blown profile of you, he or she will look up all the various gossip column items to get more background.

What you have done, if you have received regular mentions over the years, is to have built up your own life-story, brick by brick. Not all the items may be completely true, and some of them you might prefer to have kept quiet, but the overall effect at the end of the day will be that of an interesting person who has lived life to the full. If the gossip columns are the only source of fame that you achieve, of course, you will have built up a very different picture, possibly that of a ne'er do well, a parasite or something worse. But, then, if that is all the publicity you will ever get, perhaps even that is better than nothing.

Another disadvantage of appearing in gossip columns is that it is expensive and time-consuming to live the sort of life required, and unless you actually enjoy a hectic social life, you might prefer to be at work or home in bed. If you are enjoying a particularly good run of publicity, however, perhaps coinciding with the publication of a book or the screening of a television series, a few months of intensive socializing might help to promote the product, and you may find that you gain a reputation for being part of the social scene which lasts long after you have gone back to your cups of Horlicks and bed-time books.

Eventually you may become so famous that other people will be clamouring to invite you to their events in order to get some publicity for themselves out of your presence. Andy Warhol, for instance, only had to attend a party to give it a stamp of approval, and anyone who could lure Alan Sugar or Charles Saatchi out of their offices to socialize would be sure of being able to get a lot of column inches out of anything that happened at the event.

CHAPTER ELEVEN

Coping with Scandal

ANYONE WHO SETS out to be different, to stand out from the crowd and to be famous, has to accept that there is a downside to all this. The media which took such delight in building you up, could just as easily turn round, for no apparent reason, and try to tear you down. The motives, both of the media and the public, are complex. It might be that you have been exposed as a fraud or have become arrogant, and they want to take you down a peg or two. It may be that they are jealous of your success, or it may simply be that a scandalous story arises in your vicinity which smells so delicious they just can't resist rolling in it.

None of these reasons are much comfort to the politician, actor, singer, businessperson or member of the Royal Family who suddenly wakes up to find that whereas last month they were being voted most popular person of the year, today they are being smeared and vilified.

It is part of the syndrome that makes series like *Dallas* and *Dynasty* popular. Ordinary people like to be reminded, every so often, that the rich and famous are miserable too. Stories about multi-millionaires who are so mean that they put pay-phones in their houses for guests to use, reinforce all the prejudices which unsuccessful people have about successful ones. Paul Getty, at one time reported to be the richest man in the world, was always being accused of meanness. He found the accusations funny, and would feed the media with stories about himself just to build on the legend. W C Fields, famous for hating children, raised it to an art form with his one-liners about them – a characteristic which could have made him unpopular with the public became a shared joke.

The audiences you have built up will always be looking for chinks in your armour. They may want to believe that you are the greatest at what you do, but they don't want to feel duped, and they will be interested in anything naughty that you do, just as they are interested in your noble acts.

The question which you have to ask yourself, and answer absolutely truthfully, is: 'Am I doing anything which I am truly ashamed of? If my family were to find out everything that I am doing, would I be able to explain satisfactorily to them why I am doing it?'

If you are dealing in drugs, the answer is no. If you are cheating your customers out of millions of dollars, the answer is no again. If you are part of a child sex ring or a supplier of arms to South Africa, you would be well-advised not to aim for a high profile.

Look at all the things you do which might be misconstrued by the media, and be sure in your mind that you know the moral ground that you will stand on if challenged, because as soon as you hold yourself up for public approval, there is going to be someone who will challenge everything you do. It could be as simple as making large profits while denying your workforce a rise, or it could be exploiting cheap labour in the Third World or cutting down Amazonian forests.

CRISIS MANAGEMENT

It only needs a particular cause to become fashionable for you to be swiftly exposed as an exploiter of low-paid labourers, or an environmental vandal. In big business, planning for such contingencies is called 'crisis management'. Public relations companies are paid large amounts of money to draw up plans which warn the client of what might happen in certain circumstances, and how they should combat the effects on their reputation.

If you have an industrial plant which leaks a toxic substance and kills and maims tens of thousands of innocent people, you are going to have to face some heavy criticism. Likewise, an airline which forgets to check a piece of machinery, resulting in a fatal crash, or a food company which suddenly finds it has given a number of customers food poisoning, is going to find itself under attack. The same can happen to individuals.

If handled properly, most scandals can be weathered. Some can even be turned to advantage, although the advantages may be so long in coming that you might prefer not to undergo the discomfort along the way.

At the end of the 1980s, the film *Scandal* made the names of Christine Keeler and Mandy Rice Davies famous again for an event which took place in the 1960s. They were just two good-time girls, but their names were linked with the fall of a government during the Profumo affair, and they have been famous ever since.

The Watergate scandal made a number of rather grey politicians and civil servants famous enough to be able to write best-selling books on their versions of the events, not to mention the journalists who uncovered the story in the first place. More recently, the Irangate scandal under President Reagan made a star of Oliver North, a soldier who carried the can for the President with such conviction that he too ended up on the celebrity circuit, rumoured to be able to charge tens of thousands of dollars for appearances as a guest speaker at events.

These are grand scandals with intrinsic glamour and intrigue. For many people, the danger is more insidious because they have less to lose and therefore less to gain. The small-time crooks and entrepreneurs who are exposed in consumer watchdog programmes find it hard to appear anything other than seedy and furtive as they hide from the cameras behind net curtains, or turn up their collars and run to their second-hand Jaguars with the television crews hot on their heels.

They may genuinely be con-men, but it is unlikely that their crimes are as great as the ones perpetrated by the powerful people of government and big business. Such people should have started by asking themselves, 'Am I doing anything which I am truly ashamed of?' If the answer had been that they knew they were doing wrong, then they should have smiled cheerfully as the cameras and self-righteous reporters pushed through their front doors, and held up their hands, declaring it a 'fair cop'. If, on the other hand, they are convinced that they are right, then they must face down their persecutors and argue it out with them. If necessary, they should resort to the law to sue the programme-makers who seek to blacken their characters. That way they can seek to clear their names and create more publicity at the same time.

LOOKING ON THE POSITIVE SIDE

Sir James Goldsmith, before finally despairing of the anti-capitalist mood which pervaded Britain in the 1970s and moving to America, used to attack his attackers vigorously. When confronted on television by questions which he thought impertinent, he would round on his interviewer with an equally impertinent and well-researched list of questions. Feeling as confident as the television professionals under the lights, he was more than a match for them intellectually, and went on to become one of the richest and most successful people in the world. He was never in any doubt that what he was doing was right.

During major takeover battles, chief executives can expect to have their rivals hiring private detectives in attempts to dig up dirt, and the chances are that they will always find something somewhere which looks less than snow white.

There are also going to be times when companies which have so far seemed able to do no wrong suddenly hit a bad patch. If managers can meet their accusers with such good humour and common sense so that no-one listening to them or reading their words could fail to see their point of view, most people will choose to believe them. Such skills in putting a case are worth many millions of pounds to companies whose share prices are largely governed by the intangible forces of reputation and rumour.

THE ACTIONS OF OTHERS

It is sometimes more difficult for those in the public gaze to deal with scandals caused by those they love. It is relatively easy to brazen out your own mistakes, but how do you cope when a close friend is revealed by the press to be a hopeless drug addict, or when a family member is sent to prison. You may be called upon by the media to make moral pronouncements against their actions, while at the same time you will want to protect them and stand up for them.

It is a dilemma which causes pain to many celebrities, particularly as it is often their own lust for fame which has brought the media attention and pressures down on their innocent relatives and friends. There are millions of drug addicts, prostitutes and thieves in the world to whom no-one pays much attention until it is discovered that one of them has a connection with a celebrity.

Sometimes it is the actions of colleagues which cause problems. You may be working as part of a team, although you are the one with the highest profile. When disaster strikes, you are going to be the one who is held up and pilloried as the guilty party.

So what can you do to minimize the dangers of scandal to yourself, your family, your friends and your colleagues? The most important rule is 'be prepared'. Play endless 'What if?' games: 'What if my mother is caught shoplifting in Harrods?'; 'What if I am caught having an affair with someone 30 years younger than myself?'; 'What if they find out that I spent five years in prison 20 years ago?' There will always be answers to all these problems, and the main danger is that the scandals will strike you when you are least expecting them, and that you will say the wrong thing to the media when they come hammering on your door in the middle of the night, demanding to know what you have to say for yourself.

Secondly, you may actually have to be more open and honest with those around you than you would be if you were not in the public eye. If you are famous and you have something to hide, the chances are that someone will find out about it in the end. It is better to pre-empt the problem by confessing in advance, when you are still in a position of strength.

Be brave. Grasp the nettle and come out of whatever closet you are hiding in before they come to axe down the door and find you cowering in the dark.

CHAPTER TWELVE

Myth and Mystery

THERE COMES A time when a person becomes so famous that re-cognition actually begins to hamper them, both in their career and in their private life. It begins to become a bore, a chore and an embarrassment.

Showbusiness is the most obvious area where this can be a problem, but it happens in other areas as well. With the creation of the Hollywood star system and the coming of television, actors, actresses and screen personalities became known to literally millions of people. They now have more opportunities than ever to become adored or respected for the work they do on the screen, with the result that in real life they can do little but disappoint their admirers.

Comedians who have teams of scriptwriters working for them when they are making public appearances, are expected to be hysterically funny at all times; film stars and models are expected to look immaculately glamorous at all time. They are pestered and chased and have their lives made miserable by the people whose attention they were desperately craving for at the beginning of their careers.

Pop stars, at the height of their fame, often have crowd hysteria deliberately whipped up for them, with the result that they can't actually go outside their homes or hotels without armies of body-guards. It is a pressure which can only be withstood for a limited period before they want to go back to normal life, or they start to become creations of their own publicity and unable to relate to the real world.

Not only are they pursued by the public, they are also pursued by the media. Every newspaper, magazine and television company in the world wants an interview with Michael Jackson, but there is no way that he could talk to all of them, and if he did, the public would soon begin to grow tired of hearing about him – he would become 'overexposed'.

The same can happen in the business world. A person who is too successful at becoming well-known could end up being pursued for comment by the media every hour of the day, leaving him or her no time to actually run his or her business, or private life. (Of course, there's also the danger that too many interviews might also reveal that someone who is a genius at creating a multi-national corporation is actually a very dull person indeed.)

Such stars have to re-think the long-term strategy of their personal publicity, because now they have a real opportunity to turn from being someone who is merely famous into a legend, both in their own lifetime and after it.

Howard Hughes, for instance, was one of the most colourful and exotic of business figures. As a young man he directed Hollywood movies, had affairs with many of his leading ladies, designed and flew aircraft and became one of the richest men in the world. By the time he had achieved all that, he was still only half-way through his career. One way to preserve the glamour would have been to die young – like James Dean, Elvis Presley, J F Kennedy and Marilyn Monroe – but he didn't do that, he just appeared to go mad. Luckily for his public relations people, his madness took the form of re-clusiveness. No-one got to see him or talk to him, so stories were born, and proliferated. He was thought to be terrified of illness and germs, and so wouldn't have anyone in a room with him, walking everywhere on paths of disposable tissues. Some said that he stopped shaving and cutting his hair. The more fantastical the stories became, the more they were exaggerated by the media, and lapped up by the public.

On a smaller scale, Charles Saatchi and Alan Sugar have both shunned publicity, preferring to let their achievements speak for themselves. Sugar can be coaxed out of his shell occasionally to say something about the business world, and when this rare event happens, he is given all the more coverage as a result. By rationing what he has to say, he does not devalue it by making it familiar.

It is like a comedian from Vaudeville refusing to appear on television because one television show would use up his entire fund of material, material which he may have been using in the theatre all his life. Everyone who goes to see him on stage hears the jokes for the first time and can't believe how funny they are. Those people tell their friends about this genius they have discovered, and so the word spreads. Many of the longest-lasting comedians have actually rationed their appearances very carefully over the years, making sure that the public doesn't grow tired of them. If Billy Connolly agreed to make a few weekly television series, it wouldn't be long before he would lose his ability to shock and become as cosy and comfortable an institution as *The Two Ronnies*.

Familiarity will nearly always breed contempt, and famous people who fail to ration themselves will soon start to become as transparent as the most boring of old uncles and aunts found in every family. Comics who run out of new material are reduced to hosting games shows, and actresses who were once among the most glamorous women in the world are reduced to slapping policemen and having hysterics in court in order to remain on the front pages of the world media. Anyone who hasn't managed to get close to hosting a games show or to being in any newspaper can still admire the ability of these people to survive at all in such a competitive jungle. With better management and more careful forethought, however, they could perhaps manage the ends of their careers with more dignity.

The media, once they have found that you are accessible, will want to know your favourite colours and your favourite foods, and will ring you up for comment on every tiny thing that ever happens. You will begin to be expected to pontificate on every subject under the sun – just like a publicity hungry politician – and you will soon see your credibility slipping as low as the average opposition minister's.

As soon as you feel that you are getting negative reactions from the media you are talking to, or those that are talking about you, withdraw into your shell and wait to see what happens. Rumours will soon start to spread about the exotic and wonderful things which you get up to in your private life that no-one is allowed to know about. You can then choose to let the rumours grow to legendary proportions, or carefully stage an appearance on the most popular television show of the day, during which you can make a mockery of all the ridiculous stories that are being told about you!

The press can get things as wrong as they like, provided they are willing to pay the consequences of being taken to court, which the tabloids, it seems, are generally willing to do for the sake of a really good story. Anything but live television can also be edited to give the wrong impression, so you have to ensure that your appearance happens live in front of the audience – but bear in mind that the interviewer, if you have picked the wrong one, might decide to throw in a question which you weren't expecting.

As soon as you withdraw from the public gaze, like Greta Garbo and Howard Hughes, the public will remember you at the height of your powers. The oldest sort of publicity in the world is the telling of folk tales around camp fires, when generals, kings and queens of previous generations were talked about as having magical and mystical powers. They were reputed to have slayed dragons and eaten children, to have loved thousands of women, and sometimes mythical beasts as well, to have been raised by wolves or to be so beautiful they could launch a fleet of ships. Neither Cleopatra nor Helen of Troy, Homer nor Beowulf would have seemed so impressive seen perched on the surburban sofas of Terry Wogan's studio sitting room.

The Queen of England realized many years ago that she would be able to preserve her dignity better if people did not get to hear what she said under anything but the most controlled circumstances – no doubt Mrs Thatcher and a host of other politicians wish they could build their reputations under similar conditions.

BECOMING A LEGEND

To become a legend requires great luck, great skill or great deeds. Winston Churchill would probably have been just another patrician politician had there not been a war for him to win when he was an old man. Mozart was a great composer, but his much talked about private life has helped to build on the legend.

In the modern age of the media, it takes a concentrated and deliberate effort to avoid over-exposure. At some time, however, if you have been successful at every other stage in this book, you will have to decide whether or not you want to make the jump into 'legendary' status. That may mean performing a huge act – building a palace or giving millions to charity – or it may mean merely carefully husbanding and controlling your reputation, so that it will outlast you.

Critics of television say that it does not allow the audience to use their imaginations. Whereas reading and listening to the radio allow people to create their own pictures in their heads, pictures that suit their tastes and fuel their fantasies, film and television do everything for the viewer. As a result, people are able to become famous much faster. Their faces become familiar immediately and every detail about them can be known, but there can be no element of fantasy.

For the making of *Gone With the Wind*, the search for someone to play Scarlet O'Hara went on for years because no-one quite as beautiful and explosive could be found in real life. They managed eventually to find Vivien Leigh, and were lucky that they had discovered someone with the same potential to become a legend as Scarlet herself. In most cases, however, the reality of a person cannot live up to an expectation created through reputation.

Sometimes it is impossible to live up to one's own reputation for greatness, and it is better to retire into the background and let the reputation continue to work on your behalf.

CHAPTER THIRTEEN

Professional Help

ANYONE WHO IS planning to go through all the stages in this book may need some professional help along the way. It is possible to get right to the top without hiring anyone, but it is sometimes quicker and easier to use the skills of others at appropriate times. There are, however, a lot of people out there ready to take your money whether the time is appropriate or not.

PUBLIC RELATIONS CONSULTANCIES

The public relations industry is notorious for practitioners who will tell you they can make you famous when they patently can't, and who somehow manage to charge much more than you thought you originally agreed to. Having said that, there are stages in your career when good consultants will be extremely helpful at sharing the burden of self-promotion, provided you never let them take the initiative.

If you are starting to raise your profile while still working for a large company, you should immediately get to know the in-house public relations department and any consultancies working for the company. However, don't rely on them to do everything for you. Show them the articles which you would like to submit to magazines and ask them what they think. If they don't show a lot of enthusiasm or give you any encouragement, send the articles off yourself – provided there are no company rules against it, and provided you are not giving away any valuable company secrets. If, however, you like their ideas, and if you trust their judgment, you might just hand the articles over and let them do the placing. That way you will not get to know the editors yourself, but you will have become known by the public relations people, who may be the first place that editors in search of material and comments will go to.

Public relations departments are often being approached for quotes and material and their main problem is finding people within the company who are willing to give their time and able to communicate clearly. If they know that you are keen to write and speak, they will pass enquiries on to you. They will also ring you when they want a quote for a press release, particularly if your subject is a technical one and you are known to be able to explain things well in layman's terms. The public relations people attached to large companies are usually involved with the production of in-house publications and newsletters, for which they need good material. Try to find out what it is they need, and then provide it for them. That way you will increase your profile, and get some practice in writing articles to order.

If you have a good working relationship with public relations people, you will be able to suggest ideas for press releases and other activities which will increase the profile of your department, and consequently increase your profile as the spokesperson for that department.

Once you have got past the first stage, and are being asked to give speeches and write articles on a regular basis, the public relations people will be able to help you out with the services of professional speechwriters and journalists if you don't have time to prepare your own material. It is always better to write your things yourself, but there may be times when it just isn't possible to meet a deadline *and* do your full-time job, particularly if you are approached at short notice, which frequently happens.

Don't, however, let them give you something 'off the shelf', unless there really isn't time for anything else. Spend at least an hour explaining to writers what it is that you want to say, and then let them get on with it. Always read what they give you in advance and check it before it goes out. Remember, if it is wrong in any way, it is your reputation which is on the line, not theirs.

Public relations people will also be able to help you with the names of photographers, and with the creation of back-up material, such as slides for presentations. Find out what is available and make full use of it: it is in their interests to make you look good in front of outside audiences, so let them do so.

If you are in business for yourself and don't have the money to hire public relations professionals, then there is nothing that you can't do yourself, particularly with the help of an able secretary. Do not be talked into hiring an expensive public relations firm too soon: they are a luxury which you will not need for some time.

If you feel that you need guidance on how to write a press release, then take one of the many one-day courses available, or buy one of the 'how to do your own public relations' books available. If you are still not confident that your English is good enough, find someone who can write. It could be a local journalist, or someone in your company or a member of your family. Show them what you have written and ask if they think it makes sense and gives the right impression. If you are too far off the mark, then think hard about taking some lengthier training in writing, as it is going to be a vital cornerstone of your career.

It is harder to take your own pictures, and you will almost certainly need the help of a professional from the start, since amateur pictures never look like anything but what they are. If you need a photographer, ring the local paper and ask to speak to the picture desk. They are almost certain to know of some local photographers who would welcome the chance of a little extra income, and you will have made contact with someone who has experience in dealing with editors and providing them with what they want. Be sure that you know exactly what you want to achieve and how much it is going to cost (right down to the cost of prints, since that is often where charges start to mount up).

When you get to the stage where you think you can afford some professional public relations help, try first of all to find someone who will handle your work on a freelance basis. Ring the editors of the magazines that you most want to appear in and ask them if they know of anyone who would be interested in handling it. Ask them if they would be interested themselves. They will be flattered and although they probably can't help without jeopardizing their editorial integrity, they will almost certainly be able to give you a few names of people who they have found to be effective on behalf of clients in similar positions.

When public relations companies and freelancers come to quote for your business, they are going to try to charge as much as possible for the general 'handling of the account'. You can pre-empt them by being very clear about what you want. If you just want them to send out releases for you, ask how much that would cost. If you just want them to contact editors with a view to getting articles placed in special features, explain that. Don't leave any woolly areas which they can charge you a hefty retainer for. You may find some free-lancers who will be willing to accept payment only on results, i.e. you don't pay them until an article is published. Not surprisingly, this sort of practice is frowned on by the public relations estab-lishment, but you may find some hungry young freelancer who is confident enough to agree to it.

USING A CONSULTANCY

Once you have reached a stage where you do need the services of an established consultancy, try always to retain them on a project basis, something where the results are measureable and the contracts re-newable. Hire them to handle a specific book launch or publicity for some specific seminars, or to get articles on a pre-determined subject into a pre-determined list of publications. If you want a full-time ser-vice, with someone constantly promoting you and only you, it might be better to hire someone in-house whom you can train to do exactly what you want, whom you can keep an eye on and who can perform other communications tasks for you, like advertising and direct mail, if the public relations job isn't full-time.

AGENTS

There is a myth in the outside world that stars are created by agents. It started in the days of Hollywood, when agents supposedly found girls and boys working in drug stores and on garage forecourts and thrusted them into stardom. Now and then a hungry young entrepreneur will do exactly that, and the story of how it has happened will go down in showbusiness folklore, perpetuating the myth that this is how it is always done. More people are mismanaged and locked in obscurity by this sort of fumbling mismanagement than are turned into superstars. Assuming that you are not the one in a million who meets a Svengali or Professor Higgins at the beginning of your career, who is able to shape you into a star, you will have to approach the agents with something more concrete to offer.

Just as banks will never lend you money until you don't need it, agents will never build your career until you've already done all the groundwork yourself. If you sit back and hope that someone else is going to make you famous, you are doomed.

This does not mean, however, that agents can't supply services along the way, and that they can't look after your interests very efficiently once you have reached a position of eminence, and are generating enough money to make it worth their while taking an interest.

Theatrical agents are a necessity for most hopeful young actors, because that is where the jobs come from. They also provide shoulders to cry on and a financial service for people ill-equipped to handle their own accounts. Actors who seriously want to reach the top, however, will not rely on their agents to do it all for them. They will be hustling for jobs themselves, which they may then ask the agents to handle. They will be organizing their own production companies and other activities to keep the work rolling in. They will also be handling their own press relations campaign if they want it to be proactive and not merely a process of responding to requests for interviews. They will be working in conjunction with the publicity departments of television companies, film companies and theatres whenever they are involved in productions, and they will be looking for other avenues of publicity – from charity work to street theatre – when nothing else is on offer.

Likewise, literary agents have little more chance of selling the work of unknown writers than the writers themselves, and nothing like the same motivation or perseverence. Once someone is established, a literary agent can take a lot of the work out of arranging deals for books involving the sale of foreign rights, film rights and other extras. But they also slow the process down by being sticklers for everything being in contract form before they start, and often work as barriers between writer and publisher, rather than as channels of communication. There are some exceptions to the rule – the stars of the agency world who manage to do amazing deals for their clients – but then they are generally only working with clients who merit amazing deals already.

An alternative to literary agents, if you want to be sure that everything is tied up legally, is to find a firm of solicitors which is used to handling such work, and asking them to negotiate on your behalf and to check all the small print in your contracts. Publishers are just as happy to deal with a solicitor as with an agent (although they will often prefer to deal direct with the author).

Apart from public relations consultancies, there is no-one who can help you sell articles to magazines (and if you use public relations consultancies for your approaches to editors, you will not be selling the articles anyway, you will be giving them away, and paying the public relations people for the privilege).

Once you are linked up with publishers and seminar organizers, however, you are then involved with people who have as much reason to want you to be famous as you yourself have, and they will be doing all they can to help. Seminar organizers will help with any audio-visual material that you need, possibly footing the bills, or at least splitting them with you, and publishers will undertake extensive (and expensive) publicity campaigns for books if they feel the potential merits it. Once again, you have access to the public relations machine with someone else footing the bill, and you should make the most of it.

Once you have reached the upper levels of your career, and you are able to start generating higher levels of income, the more skilful and valuable managers and agents will become interested in you. Mark McCormack is the most visible (having followed the fame trail himself), but there are many others who are able to do deals on behalf of clients which are far bigger and more important than anything the clients could have done for themselves.

These people can organize sponsorship and advertising deals which will set a client up for life. They can organize investments and international deals which turn stars into legends, and provide financial security on a grand scale. They are, however, very unlikely to spot you on the way up and invest time and effort into promoting you themselves. They will wait for you to poke your head above the crowd and then they will start making their offers.

GROOMING AND TRAINING

Giving advice on grooming and training is not a new profession, but with the increasing importance of television in all walks of life, it is a growing one. The problem is that it is all so much a question of personal taste. A professional adviser, used to dressing actors and actresses, for instance, might not appreciate how uncomfortable and self-conscious someone in another profession will feel if they are asked to wear something radically different from their usual clothes, or to change their hairstyle dramatically.

The best way to develop a style of dress and grooming is to study magazines and role models, decide what look you want to adopt, and then go to the shops, armed with pictures, and ask them to see how close they can get to that style. The same can be done at the hairdresser.

One area where training might be very useful is in voice projection and general public speaking skills. A drama coach who can help you to speak more clearly and dynamically is going to be worth investing in. Anything that makes you feel more confident when you are on the stage or in front of the cameras, and cuts down nervous tension, will speed your rise to eminence. Speaking to cameras, in particular, with the sort of forced 'naturalness' which that requires, is a different skill from standing up on a platform and reacting to the audience.

If you work for a large company, it should be able to provide you with some training for presenting and lecturing, but it may not think of training you to perform in front of the cameras unless you have already reached a senior management level, one which might involve you in talking to network television. If you show yourself as keen to learn, however, the chances are that your company will include you in a training scheme.

If you are in business on your own, you may be able to persuade the director or producer of whatever video project you are involved in to give you some coaching before the event. If they don't have the time, they should be able to recommend a good training establishment.

Summary

THERE ARE TWO fundamental rules to becoming well-known. Firstly, you must do a good job. Whether you are working as a cog in a giant company, or are a star of a television show, make sure that you are supremely skilful at what you do, because otherwise you are going to be found out.

Next, you have to let people know just how good you are. If no-one knows you are a genius, then you might as well not make the effort to be one, because you will never be given opportunities which will stretch you and use up all your capabilities.

If you are working within a large organization, you may well have to learn to handle corporate politics on your way to the top. There are always going to be people who want to slow you down. Your boss is not going to want you to shine too brightly, if it makes him or her look dim by comparison. You are going to have to be tactful and look for ways of showing your skills to your boss' bosses which also show your boss up in a good light.

Someone who is too obviously ambitious can end up being very unpopular. Other people feel that they are being looked down on and left behind. Perhaps they feel envious or perhaps they just don't think it's very tasteful to be so boastful about one's own achievements. If you have natural tact and charm – both ingredients which will speed your climb to the top anyway – you will be able to excel at what you do without putting other people's noses out of joint. Always try to get permission for writing articles and giving speeches if the company rules demand it, but plan carefully how to do it so as to avoid having the permission refused. If you have approached an institution which is organizing a seminar and asked if you can speak, it is better that you tell your boss that you have been approached by them rather than the other way round.

It might also be an idea to ask if you can interview your boss to gather material for the speech – he or she is unlikely to say no – and you could then ask if you can interview the boss' boss as well. That way everyone knows that you are giving a speech and all the people who matter are behind you. You will also have been able to build up more in-depth information to be used as background, and will be speaking with the authority of senior management.

The next rule on the road to high visibility is to be as interesting as possible. As you start to achieve more, you will find that you

SUMMARY

become interesting to people simply through the job that you hold and your success at doing it. Donald and Ivana Trump became a king and queen of New York society because of their outrageously high profile success as property developers, financiers and hoteliers. Even those who don't like their style have to admit that they are interesting at the moment, which means that they can make contacts at any level they like, which leads to them being even more successful and attractive to other achievers.

People like to meet interesting and successful people because they see themselves reflected in the glory. Hostesses like to fill their parties with successful actors, businesspeople, authors, politicians and anyone else who will help them to shine. So if you want to be invited, work hard, let people see the results of that hard work, and don't let them forget it!

Index

advertisements 85–6, 104
adviser to readers, becoming an 17
agents 103–4
ambition 106
Archer, Jeffrey 79
audience, finding an 34
audio–cassettes 45–6

Beaton, Cecil 76
Becker, Boris 48
Benn, Anthony 24
Blanc, Raymond 26, 48
Blanchard, Ken 62
Bond, Alan 75
books, writing 61–73
Borg, Bjorn 81
Boyle, Katie 85
Branson, Richard 73, 75, 78, 79, 84
broadcasting, structure of 54
Brynner, Yul 84
Bucknell, Barry 53
business confrontations 24–5
business press 17
by–lines 10, 18

captions for photographs 14
Cartland, Barbara 79
celebrities 59, 75
Cleese, John 55
clothes 81–5
colleagues 95
colour 83
comment columns 5
communication 29–32
company spokesperson, becoming 13

conference organizers 15
conferences 73
confidentiality 12
confirmation of quotes 12
confrontation 24–5
Connolly, Billy 97
Conran, Terence 78
consultants 39
consumer media 16–25
contact lists 11
context, being quoted out of 12
Cooper, Henry 22, 36
copies of articles 15
Coward, Noel 84
Craddock, Fanny 53
Crawford, Joan 25
crisis management 93–4
criticism 8
curriculum vitae 42

Daniels, Paul 84
Davis, Bette 25
Davis, George 24
Day, Robin 84
deadlines 6
Dean, James 97
De Lorean, John 74, 80
De Savary, Peter 75, 78
diary columns 3
dress *see* clothes

editors, meeting the needs of 2
Egan, John 74
events organizers 34
Everidge, Dame Edna 85

face-to-face meetings 8
facts and figures, for

publication 3
familiarity 97
family 95
Fenton, John 36, 37
Fields, W C 92
first impressions 80
Floyd, Keith 53
Fonda, Jane 55
Forbes, Malcolm 88-9
Ford, Anna 89
Ford, Henry 57
Forsyth, Frederick 85
Forte, Lord 24
free publications 16
friends 95
Frost, David 53

Garbo, Greta 98
Garland, Judy 79
Geldof, Bob 23, 86
Getty, Paul 92
gimmicks 84-5
glamour 75
Goldsmith, James 25, 94
good causes 19, 23-4
Goodhew, Duncan 84
gossip columns 87-8
Grade, Lew 84
Grade, Michael 84
Grant, Russell 53
grooming 104-5
Guccione, Bob 89
guest appearance, 52
guest speaker, being a 33-8
Guild, Tricia 76, 78
'gurus' 38

hairstyle 84
Hall, Jerry 76
Halpern, Ralph 83
Hanson, Lord 25
Harty, Russell 58
Harvey Jones, John 84
Hawking, Stephen 48
Hefner, Hugh 89

Hicks, David 76
hosting 89-91
Hughes, Howard 97, 98

Iacocca, Lee 57
ideas for stories 3-4
image
  creating 80-6
  selling 85-6
industry source, becoming an 3
information for speeches 39
interesting, how to be 77-9
interests, using your 26-7
interviews 44

Jackson, Michael 85, 96
Jagger, Mick 76
Jameson, Derek 53
John, Elton 82, 85

Kalms, Stanley 25
Keeler, Christine 93
Kennedy, John F 76, 97
Kiam, Victor 56
Laker, Freddie 74
layout, magazine 5
Lee, Albert 70
legend, becoming a 99
Leigh, Vivien 99
Levin, Bernard 26
Liberace 82
life history, sketch of 78
lifestyle, using your 74-9
local media 16-20

MacGregor, Ian 24
magazines 4
maintaining fame 79
Martin, James 29-32, 36, 37, 40, 63
material
  for articles 7
  for speeches 32, 38-40
Maxwell, Robert 24, 57, 89
McCormack, Mark 63, 86, 104

media
  consumer 16–25
  local 16–20
  national 20–5
  trade 1–15
men-only magazines 17
Minelli, Liza 84
modesty 58
Monroe, Marilyn 97
Moran, Diana 83
Moss, Stirling 22, 85
Most, Mickie 75
Murdoch, Rupert 24

national media 20–5
Newman, Nanette 85
newsletters 39
news stories 3, 13, 90
Niven, David 85
Nixon, Richard 78
North, Oliver 93

Onassis, Aristotle 81
originality 38
over-exposure 99

Palin, Michael 73
Parkinson, Norman 76
parties
  giving 89
  going to 88
payment
  for articles 9
  for speeches 35–6
Perot, Ross 70
persistence 16
personality 53
personal stories 76–7
Peters, Tom 62
photographs 13–14
photo opportunities 25
physical appearance 81–5
Picasso, Paloma 85
Powell, Enoch 24
Presley, Elvis 97

pictures 13–14, 101
press
  boom 2
  business 17
  coverage 41–2
  creating opportunities for the 77
  officer, appointing a 58
  releases 11, 90, 101
private life 57–8
professional help 100–5
props 32
publicity 10, 21–2, 49, 58, 68
publicity stunts 21
public relations consultancies 12, 100–2
public speaking 29–42
publishers
  approaching 65–8
  biographies 72
  ghost-writers 71–2
  replies from 67–8
  requirements of 64–5
  sponsorship 69–71
  'vanity' publishing 69–71
publishing a book 61–73

quote source, becoming a 3, 10–11

radio
  broadcast taping 45
  international 45
  interviews 44
  local 43–4
  national 44–5
  producers 44
  transcripts, adaptation of 45
readership, finding a 61–2
rejection, coping with 7
relaxed, appearing 51
reliability 5–6
research 22
Rice Davies, Mandy 94
Roberts, Wess 70

Roddick, Anita 78
Roussos, Demis 82
Rowland, Tiny 24
royalties 66
rumours 75

Saatchi, Charles 91, 97
Sassoon, Vidal 81
Saville, Jimmy 84
scandal, coping with 79, 92–5
Scargill, Arthur 24, 84
scripts for speeches 35
selling stories 7
seminar organizers 15, 38
seminars 37, 73
series adviser, becoming a 53
Smith, Roger 70
social circle 88
speaking in public see public
  speaking
specialization 26
special reports 8
spectacles 85
speech problems 52
spokesperson, being a 19
sponsorship 55, 69, 104
status 10
Stewart, Jackie 22, 85
style
  speaking 33
  writing 18
Sugar, Alan 26, 91, 97
surveys 22

talked about, being 87–91
target audience 4–5
Taylor, Dennis 85
teaching 40
telephone interviews 12
television
  advertisements 56–7

behind the screen 53–4
cashing in 57–60
comment 49
company internal 48
current affairs programmes 50
independent producers 54
major channels 49
mistakes on 51
news 49–50
payment 50
satellite and cable 56
series adviser, becoming a 53
studio discussions 50
training for 50–2
video magazines 54–5
Thrower, Percy 53
Toleman, Ted 75–6
'trade mark', developing a 80
trade media 1–15
training 32–3, 40, 100–5
Trump, Donald 107
Trump, Ivana 107

Unique Selling Point,
  developing a 26–8

vanity publishing 69
videos, training and education
  48, 55

Warhol, Andy 2, 91
Waterman, Bob 62
Welles, Orson 85
Wilde, Oscar 12
Wogan, Terry 98
women's media 17
workshops 59
writer's block 6–7
writers
  contacting 11
  freelance 11